SECRETS YOUR CREDITORS DON'T WANT YOU TO KNOW

Know Your Rights, Eliminate Debt, and Restore Your Good Name

WADE TORKELSON
THE #1 AUTHORITY ON DEBT RELIEF

SECRETS
YOUR CREDITORS
DON'T WANT YOU TO KNOW

Know Your Rights, Avoid Bankruptcy and Foreclosure,
Eliminate Debt, and Restore Your Good Name

INCLUDES: STUDENT LOAN, DEBT SETTLEMENT,
LOAN CONSOLIDATION INFORMATION–AND MORE!

WADE TORKELSON
with
MARK A. CAREY, ESQ.
LARRY R. TAYLOR, Ph.D.

Secrets Your Creditors Don't Want You to Know

©2022 SADM Holdings, Inc.

All rights reserved. No part of this book may be used or reproduced by any means, graphic, electronic, or mechanical, including photocopying, recording, taping or by any information storage retrieval system without the written permission of the publisher, except in the case of brief quotations embodied in critical articles and reviews.

Cover and interior design: Dino Marino

Paperback ISBN: 979-8-9853405-1-8

eBook ISBN: 979-8-9853405-0-1

SPECIAL INVITATION

Be sure to get access to the book's bonuses at:

Jubi.com/book-bonuses

TABLE OF CONTENTS

INTRODUCTION: SECRETS FROM AN INDUSTRY INSIDER i
    An Insider's Take on the Credit Industry iii
    My First Foray into Debt... iv
    Why I Want to Help You v
    An Assessment Creates Real Solutions.. vi

CHAPTER ONE: THE RIGHT MINDSET 1
    The System Continues to Fail Us as Consumers 1
    How Did You Get Here?.. 3
    Getting Your Mindset Right for the Journey Ahead.................................. 6
    How to Think like a Bank Regarding Hardships....................................... 8
    Acknowledging and Assessing Your Situation 9
    Your Loan Health: A Personal Assessment 10
    Accepting the Cold Hard Truth:
    You Will Have to Deal with Your Creditors 12
    Understanding Your Hardship and Creating Your Game Plan 13

CHAPTER TWO: AN OVERVIEW OF THE CONSUMER DEBT PROCESS 15
    The History of Credit 15
    In the Game of Credit, Knowing Your Opponent Is Key 16
    What Your Credit Score Means and How It Is Figured........................ 18
    Credit Can Heal Over Time.. 19

Types of Active and Passive Debt 20
A Well-Rounded Perspective on the Debt Dynamic 22
Thin-File Clients 23
The System Is Rigged Against You 24
How Credit Reports Work 26
Credit Is a Status Symbol 27
The Benefits of Credit Cards 28

CHAPTER THREE: INSIDER SECRETS 30
Credit Is a Trap 30
Perks Aren't Perks 33
How the Collections Process Works 34
How Lenders Look at You and Treat Your Debt 35
The Truth About Lawsuits 36
Old Debt Never Really Dies 36
Parking Debt 37
Hardship Stories Aren't Hard 38
Whatever You Do, Don't Lie 41
Will You Get Sued? 41
Who Gets Paid First? 42
The Hierarchy of Payback 43

CHAPTER FOUR: CHOOSING YOUR PATHWAY FORWARD 44
Look at Yourself the Way a Creditor Does 44
Your Mindset Is the Most Critical Ingredient of Your Success 47
Delinquent Credit Works in Buckets 48
Stop, Drop, and Budget 49
Determining Your Assets and Income 51
You Have Freedom of Choice 53

CHAPTER FIVE: LOAN CONSOLIDATION 55
Do You "Walk on Water?" 55
Is Loan Consolidation Right for You? 56
Comparing the Positives and Negatives of Loan Consolidation 57
When Is Loan Consolidation the Right Option? 59
A Word About High Interest Rates 60
Who Is to Blame? 60

CHAPTER SIX: CREDIT COUNSELING AND DEBT MANAGEMENT 62
Portfolios over People 62
Are You Eligible for an Early Charge-Off? 64
Comparing the Positives and Negatives of Credit Counseling 65
Positives of Credit Counseling 65
Negatives of Credit Counseling 66
If it Sounds Too Good to Be True 67

CHAPTER SEVEN: DEBT SETTLEMENT 69
The Debt Settlement Process 70
Knowing the Ins and Outs of Debt Can Save You Time, Money, and Sanity 71
Don't Fall for Fear 72
When Is the Right Time to Settle? 73
Multiple Debts Between Credit Cards 74
Calling Your Creditors 75
Debt Settlement Companies Can Do Better 77
Comparing the Positives and Negatives of Debt Settlement 79
Positives of debt settlement: 79
Negatives of debt settlement: 79
Bankruptcy and Lawsuits 79
Borrowing 80

CHAPTER EIGHT: WHAT IS BANKRUPTCY? 82
How Did Bankruptcy Originate? 82
What Is a Chapter 13 Bankruptcy? 84
What Is a Chapter 7 Bankruptcy? 85
What You Should Know (But Probably Don't)
Before You File Bankruptcy 85
Negatives of Bankruptcy 87
Positives of Bankruptcy 90
When Do I Know It Is Time to File Bankruptcy? 90

CHAPTER NINE: SO, YOU THINK YOU WANT
TO SETTLE YOUR OWN DEBT? 92
Inside a Debt Settlement Department 93
The Debt Life Cycle Is One Tricky Puzzle 94
A Debt Collector's Goal Is to Make Money
While Separating You from Yours 96
Debt Validation 97
A Defined Debt Strategy 99
Step 1: Getting Your Mind Right for the Fight 100
Step 2: Managing Multiple Creditors 101
Dave's Debt Snowball 101
Positives of Doing It Yourself 102
Negatives of Doing It Yourself 103
How Do I Know If I Should Try to Settle My Own Debt? 104

CHAPTER TEN: KNOWLEDGE IS POWER 107
Banks Will Make Money Off You Either Way 108
First-Party Creditor (The Original Creditor) 110
Third-Party Creditor (A Collection Agency) 110
How Debt Collection Agencies Work 112
How to Know When Your Rights Have Been Violated 114
FACTS: Your Account is Currently in Collections. 115

The Fair Credit Reporting Act (FCRA) 118
Why Is Your Credit Report and Credit Score So Important? 119
What Is the FCRA, and What Are Your Rights Under It? 119
Common Violations of the FCRA 120
The Telephone Consumer Protection Act (TCPA) 123
Debt Collection Calls 123
Signs That a Call Is an Autodialed Robocall 123
What You Can Do to Stop Robocalls 124
Frequently Asked Questions About Debt Collections 125

CHAPTER ELEVEN: FINANCIAL WELLNESS IS MORE ABOUT YOUR SELF-WORTH THAN NET WORTH 131

Financial Stress Can Impact Your Mental Health 132
Modern Man Processes Emotional Responses
in the Form of a Physical Reaction 134
The Link Between Emotional Wealth and Financial Health 136
Nutritional Considerations to Minimize
the Effects of Financial Stress 139
How Food Affects Mood 139
Foods that help you be healthy 139
Foods to Avoid 140
Foods & Nutrients to Include 140
Tips for Effectively Navigating Financial Stress 141

CHAPTER TWELVE: SOLVING YOUR STUDENT DEBT PROBLEMS 146

The Easiest Money 148
You Are Not Alone—Who Has Student Loan Debt? 148

SECTION 1: UNDERSTANDING YOUR STUDENT DEBT 150

Student Loan Debt Is More Complex Than You Might Think 150
Federal Student Loans 150
Private Student Loans 151

The Consolidation Mills and Refinancing...152
The Pandemic Pause..154
Assessing Your Numbers and Collecting Your Loan Data.................155
In Trouble: What to Pay First?..156
Bankruptcy and Settlement of Student Debt.......................................156

SECTION II: THE PSYCHOLOGY BEHIND YOUR STUDENT DEBT 158
Facing the Problem..158
Your Numbers and Mindset 158
Getting a Partner to Help..160
The Mental and Emotional Dimensions of Student Debt 160
Find Professional Help!..161
Vetting Your Financial Advisor for Help with Student Loans
(and Financial Management) 163
The 10 Critical Questions to
Ask Before You Choose a Student Loan Advisor................................164
In Summary...168
The Cost of Real Help...168

**CONCLUSION: HEALING YOUR MINDSET
WITH MONEY AND YOUR CREDIT..171**
It's Never Too Late to Salvage Your Own Relationship with Money.171
Teach Your Kids About Money...172

ABOUT THE AUTHOR...174

ACKNOWLEDGMENTS...175

APPENDIX:..176

GLOSSARY OF TERMS..178

INDEX..184

INTRODUCTION

SECRETS FROM AN INDUSTRY INSIDER

A few weeks ago, I was standing in line behind a guy at the coffee shop. I wasn't paying much attention to him until I heard the barista whisper that his card had been declined. He quickly searched through his wallet for another, and the back of his neck turned bright red as he held his breath until that one cleared. Then, with his head down, he left the shop without making eye contact with the rest of us. I can't imagine he enjoyed his latté much.

But I bet he was back the next day.

As an industry insider who believes consumers are getting screwed over, I instinctively recognize the signs of someone drowning in money trouble and instantly try to analyze how they got there.

It starts with a missed payment and maybe a polite phone call to the credit card company, begging them to remove the late fee. After all, you've never done this before, and you promise it will never happen again. Soon, you're paying the absolute minimum monthly payment toward your debt, swearing you'll throw more money at it next month. You've got no reserves to save you when unexpected expenses arise, and before you know it, you're applying for a higher credit limit and yet another credit card.

What's the worst that can happen? You'll figure it out next month.

In the meantime, you enjoy your daily coffee shop latté and a slice of lemon pound cake if you feel like treating yourself, dinner with friends where you generously offer to foot the bill, and expensive shoes to wear to work because "I've got to *look* money to *make* money." And when the first creditor call comes, you answer and explain the mistake: You simply forgot to pay, you'll send the payment immediately, and it will never happen again.

But it does.

The calls continue, becoming more aggressive and threatening. "If you don't pay," they warn, "we'll pursue legal action." You stop answering your phone, but the messages stack up. "If you don't pay," they bully, "we're contacting your employer and garnishing your wages. Won't that be humiliating?" Then comes the terrorizing message you've dreaded since this nightmare began: "We have no other choice. We're sending the sheriff to your house."

It infuriates me that we've all been programmed by the credit card companies to play their game. We need credit to get the things in life we're expected to have: a car, a home, a vacation twice a year, and a bigger TV than the one our neighbor just bought. Credit is physically enjoyable, too. Each new purchase we couldn't otherwise afford stimulates our brains to release hefty doses of dopamine, the pleasure messenger. It's basic biology. And the credit card companies know that and use it to their advantage.

That happiness trigger starts early in life. Have you ever wondered why candy and cut-rate toys are stocked a foot-and-a-half off the ground at the checkout line? That setup gives wild toddlers with no impulse control the option of begging their parent for a treat to bribe their continued happiness or utterly losing their minds when they're told no. We never really evolve past that instinctual choice structure, do we?

Purchases make us happy and denying ourselves does not. So, we keep making purchases because we only live once, right?

Since you're reading this book, you've likely experienced the extreme stress of managing your debt and creditor intimidation. You may be in the middle of it right now. And you're probably panicking about what to do next. Sound familiar?

But first . . . pause for just a moment. Take a deep breath. We're going to get through this together.

AN INSIDER'S TAKE ON THE CREDIT INDUSTRY

How can I be so sure? Like I mentioned, I'm an industry insider, and I have been through it all. In the 1990s, I found myself in debt with no clue how I'd gotten so deep so quickly. Without any knowledge of the options available to consumers experiencing debt, I discovered the harmful information gap between creditors, collectors, and the rest of us. And since 1999, I've spent my career innovating ways to shrink that gap and help the consumers save money, save time, educate themselves, get out of debt, and avoid bankruptcy—unless that's the only possible option available. And sometimes it is. But it isn't the end of the world.

Now, a question. Did you read your credit card agreement that came in the envelope with your card, which was legally activated at the same time as that card?

"Why would I read that?" You're probably shaking your head. "It's standard stuff, isn't it?"

It is. You're right.

Credit card companies have strict rules and regulations. The Federal Deposit Insurance Corporation (FDIC) and the Office of the Comptroller of the Currency (OCC) are in charge of how the banks handle consumers and credit cards. There's even an FDIC manual called the *Credit Card Activity Manual*, consisting of twenty sections, a supremely helpful glossary, and two appendices of legalese that regulates every rule by which every bank must abide.

The credit card companies, banks, and collectors all have rules they must legally follow. *They're regulated*, you might think. *That must mean the system is honest and equitable, right?*

Not so fast. When only one side knows the rules of the game, it's not a fair match. To enter into credit agreements at the same level as our opponent, we've got to learn the rules, and then we've got to practice them daily.

Otherwise, we'll lose. We could lose *everything*.

Secrets Your Creditors Don't Want You to Know is our playbook. It's different from the other debt advice in that I'm not interested in offering generic, one-size-fits-all solutions. Those never worked for me, and they may not be much help to you. Debt looks different for each of us and is dependent on our specific circumstances, hardships, and goals. You have options, and I want to enlighten you about all of them.

Maybe you're young and realize you've been taught nothing about establishing smart financial habits, building a strong credit profile, and maintaining a solid payment history. Or you could be comfortably carrying debt but never coming close to paying it off, making payment after payment without contributing to your kids' education, emergency funds, or your retirement. Maybe peers look at you, impressed by your advanced career, enviable home, new cars every few years, and kids who attend elite, high-priced schools, but they don't know the financial strain you're experiencing and what that strain is doing to your health and your relationships. And what about those who've reached retirement age and are still struggling to service their debt on a fixed income, unable to enjoy the relaxed twilight years they were all eagerly anticipating? It pains me to tell you that those seventy and above are in the fastest-growing category of credit consumers.

No matter your circumstance, we need to even your playing field. That begins with knowing the specific options that are available to you.

Let me repeat that: *Your. Specific. Options.*

MY FIRST FORAY INTO DEBT

I've always been interested in the creditor's mindset, the collector's impetus, and the consumer's education because I've been in each of those positions at certain points in my life. My interest started accidentally when a former partner added me to her maxed-out credit cards.

"Why would you do that?" I was horrified.

"I thought I was doing you a favor," she answered. "You need credit, don't you? And we're married. This is what married people do."

I knew it was bad when I went to the grocery store with her and watched her pay with *three cards*.

"Put fifty on this one, thirty on this one, and the rest on this one," she instructed the cashier, as I suddenly realized the debt pain I was about to incur.

The calls soon began, evolving from kind reminders to horror-film tactics pretty quickly. They threatened to come to my place of work and inform my boss and coworkers of my deadbeat status.

I hesitated before turning into my driveway every day after work, searching for the sheriff they warned would be waiting to arrest me and confiscate my home and all my belongings.

"You can't scare me, and you can't make me feel pathetic," I told them. "This isn't even my debt."

None of it made sense to me. I was so stressed and angry, and *it wasn't even my debt*. They didn't care. Those creditors kept up their harassment through our divorce and long after, until one day, I hit the ATM, and my money wasn't available. They had levied *my account*.

I believed the creditors when they told me bankruptcy was my only option. What else could I do *but* file for bankruptcy? I panicked and did just that.

It turns out, that was not my only option. I still regret it. And I vowed soon after to never be in that position again.

WHY I WANT TO HELP YOU

In my long career, I've done it all when it comes to credit. I've owned companies that were in the business of debt buying and debt settlement. I've even owned a company dedicated to debt collections. I've filed for bankruptcy, recovered, and built my credit back up. I've even created software programs that help consolidate debt.

That is *why* I know the industry so well. I've been on both ends, was swallowed whole, and came out on the other side with insider knowledge that consumers should know but don't.

I think it is important for people to understand the debt buying process. And I think it's important to understand what credit is and isn't, as well as what it can do for you *and to you*.

It's also important for everyone to understand that people find themselves in debt all the time. You aren't a bad person if you have debt. Sure, sometimes you may have managed your money poorly and overspent. But most of the time, unexplained events happened, and through no fault of your own, you had to put a purchase or three on a credit card.

And now, you sit there as a consumer, being scared to death when you owe someone money. The banks are big, after all, and they are going to come and crush you and intimidate you and make you feel like crap until you cave in and pay them back in full—even if you have to sell everything you own. That's not true, you know, but it's often how people *feel*.

You need to understand that Big Brother operates in debt all day long, and so do many big companies. You deserve the same rights as large corporations. The first step to freedom is through education and assessing where you are, so you'll know where to go next.

AN ASSESSMENT CREATES REAL SOLUTIONS

On paper, you may model as the perfect candidate for bankruptcy until I learn you work in the government, military, or another agency where you've earned a security clearance. If you file for bankruptcy, you're done. You will lose your standing in your organization. Deciding to file for bankruptcy would have a devastating impact on your life.

Let's say you're in sales, traveling weekly throughout your territory to meet with clients and advance your relationship. If you file for bankruptcy and lose your credit cards, you won't be able to book a flight, check into a hotel, rent a car, or maintain your job in any capacity. Imagine being forced to rent a car with a debit card; they'll take 150% of your anticipated charges and lock up your balance for up to thirty days.

There's a better way. When I look at solutions, I start with an assessment.

- **Tell me about your financial situation.** I want the down and dirty. How much do you make? What do you roughly spend to run your household every month? What are your current debt obligations?

- **What got you into this situation?** Did you or a loved one have a medical emergency that caused debt? Are you covered in student loans? Did you use a credit card to cover an expense and have been unable to pay it off?

- **Describe your state of affairs.** Are you a single mom? Are you married? How old are you? What kind of job do you have? Do you feel confident that you'll still have that job or be promoted in the next six months? Is that job in jeopardy? Is it shift work? Is it full-time work? Is it part-time work? Do you have kids? How old are your kids?

- **What are your goals and expectations?** Many consumers want to erase their current financial issues and start over immediately with a brand-new credit card. Many vow to never touch credit again. I've seen it all, and I have solutions for everything in between.
- **What sacrifices are you willing to make?** Whatever option you ultimately choose, there will be some pain, some disruption, and sacrifices that you have to accept and make.

That last point is crucial to understanding what's involved on your end—a commitment to follow the plan we put into action, even if you know it's going to hurt a little. Okay, it might hurt a lot. There is no quick fix. It will take time, effort, and some mental stamina. But you're not alone.

There are several options for getting out of debt—including loan consolidation, credit counseling and debt management, debt settlement, bankruptcy, and choosing to settle your debt without assistance—and one of these options is best for you, regardless of your current circumstances. No matter what, know that you'll get through it. And when you're on the other side, you'll have better financial knowledge, less stress, and better credit!

Beware of anyone who tells you it'll be easy. They're lying. It's part of their sales pitch.

But I can assure you that when it's over, it'll be worth it.

(Also, if you're in a huge hurry, feel free to jump to chapter four to discover your options.)

What You Can Do Right Now

- Make sure you have access, whether electronic or on paper, to all of your current financial documents, including bank accounts and statements, credit card statements, and all other lines of credit or current debts.
- If you're anxious, confused, or angry, that's okay. No matter how you got here, there's a way forward that will work for you.

CHAPTER ONE

THE RIGHT MINDSET

Having the right mindset is putting yourself in an equal position with your creditors by gaining proper knowledge. Remember, you are a tiny wheel in the machine. To put it into perspective, you are one little account within trillions of dollars of debt.

THE SYSTEM CONTINUES TO FAIL US AS CONSUMERS

I've said it before, but it bears repeating. The credit card industry has programmed us, and the system is failing us.

If you listen to the barrage of targeted ads and commercials, you'd think it's impossible to make it through life without a credit score and a perfect one at that. Credit-scoring psychology is powerful.

We blindly enter into these credit agreements as a rite of passage without learning the first thing about establishing healthy money practices or developing our financial acumen. Our parents may not have known how to manage their own money, so they had no advice to pass down to us. Our school systems certainly don't teach us financial literacy. And the banks and credit card companies aren't going to teach us how to manage our resources responsibly.

No! If we want to achieve any aspect of the American Dream—from the house that might be a tad bigger than we need, an enviably new luxury car,

[margin note: necessary vs. unnecessary]

or a higher social status—unless we have wads of cash, we have no choice but to add debt to get it.

It's ridiculously easy to fall into a hole. It's even easier to stay there when there's no possible means to climb back out.

The system and our mindsets and beliefs around debt and credit are failing us. I can't change the system, though I tried. So, my goal is to shift your mindset. Although you may be in debt, you are not a bad person. You can resolve your debt and get your life back!

The first thing we have to do to combat this is get rid of the idea of good debt and bad debt. I don't like those phrases. There are certain types of debt that may be necessary and some that are unnecessary. One example of a necessary debt is a mortgage. We all need a place to live, and most of us aren't going to be able to save up $350,000 to buy a home outright. But you do not need a brand-new car, which depreciates 25–30% as soon as you drive it off the lot. That's a prime example of unnecessary debt.

Now is the best time to reevaluate your relationship with money. Remember these key tips as we work through all of the options and angles available to you as you assess your current situation:

- **Be honest about your financial situation.** It's one of the most painful parts of shifting your mindset to accept your current reality, but it must be addressed. Start by asking yourself how much you owe and how much you can pay.

- **You're not a bad person because you're in debt.** Creditors actually use the term "deadbeat" to describe those who miss payments, and it's easy to buy into their hostile narrative. Just know that they're following a written script that's intended to *guilt* you into paying your debt, so don't take it personally. Chances are, the customer service agent on the other end of the line is in debt, too.

- **Remind yourself why you're in this mess.** The credit industry is designed to benefit creditors, *not* consumers. Understanding what you're up against is crucial in ensuring your ultimate success.

- **Financial instincts are taught.** If you never learn about finances and money management in school or from successful family members, how can you possibly expect to perform well in the credit and debt industry? You can't.

- **Look at yourself like a business.** This can be a hugely positive shift in perspective! When a business gets in trouble, they don't ignore it and hope it magically disappears, and they definitely don't feel ashamed. They simply restructure their debt. Consumers can do that, too.
- **Take a deep breath.** No, really. You need to pause and consider your next move. People under great stress who've made poor financial decisions will continue to make poor financial decisions because they're panicked. Set yourself up for success by being as level-headed as you can be.
- **Don't fall for the quick fix.** When you speak with creditors, credit counselors, and debt settlers, try not to be so stressed about getting out of your debt drama that you'll accept any solution—the first or the worst—with a deep sigh of relief. Don't do that.
- **Every move has a consequence.** The first phone calls you'll receive when your problems begin are usually from unsecured creditors. They're going to apply pressure so you'll make payments to an unsecured credit card rather than continuing your car loan payments. Suddenly, the car gets repossessed, and you have no way to get to work, eventually losing your livelihood. Be smart about your decisions.
- **Take a deep breath.** Yes, I already said that, but you probably need another one. Changing your mindset around debt and the steps required to pay it down is hard work. But you can do it. And you'll get through this.

The more you can keep your self-talk positive and remember that you'll eventually get through the process, the better off you'll be.

HOW DID YOU GET HERE?

When it comes to debt, everyone has a different story, but they all end up in the same predicament. Each person has a different spin on a similar situation.

When I owned a debt settlement agency, we trained our customer service representatives on what to say when the consumer called. We instructed our employees to *listen* to the consumer because they wanted to tell someone the story of how they got into debt. It was a confession of sorts. The situations that people get themselves into are so varied. But the truth is that they all have a common thread of debt where the money simply ran out.

We heard a multitude of stories, and some were truly heartbreaking. While many consumers experience medical reasons for going into debt, there are also plenty of unforeseen circumstances that lead to unpaid bills, such as issues with a car or a house, a divorce, or a job loss.

A caller would often begin by sharing their circumstances. "I was in a car accident, and the medical bills pushed me over the edge. I've barely been keeping my head above water just making minimum payments, and now I just can't do it anymore. I was using my cards to survive, paying my utilities and daily expenses. I didn't realize the interest was climbing every day." When they realized that by only making minimum payments, they were not making a dent in the amount they owed, they began using credit cards to make payments, and they didn't know how to get out of that cycle.

Inevitably, a consumer would come to realize they didn't make enough money to pay off the new credit card debt they were accruing to pay off the original debt. But they didn't feel they had any other choice than to get *yet another credit card*, possibly one with a lower interest rate, to pay off the first credit card. In that situation, the person primarily lived on cards instead of cash.

Other times, we'd hear a story about an unmarried couple who decided they wanted to buy a house together. They started sharing credit to make the big purchase, loading up on debt together. Then when the relationship soured, they would split up, leaving a trail of destruction that they had to unwind and sort through.

Sometimes people are just one unexpected circumstance away from the cliff.

The following are some of the most common reasons for people to get into debt:

- Didn't understand compound interest
- Job loss
- Divorce
- Medical situation, procedure, or diagnosis
- A death in the family

- "I just got crazy with my credit cards."
- Innocent ignorance (didn't know they had to make more than the minimum payment)
- Robbing Peter to pay Paul (getting another credit card to pay off the first credit card)
- Natural disaster
- House or car problem (refrigerator went out, needed new tires, etc.)
- Taxes
- Student loans (student loan payments were so high they couldn't keep up)
- Fertility treatments
- Adoption
- Gambling and other addictions
- Plastic surgery
- Veterinarian bills
- Starting a business

Sometimes, as I experienced, people would make purchases on a credit card and hide it from their spouses. But mostly, we saw people from all income brackets using cards to get themselves through the month. *No one is immune.*

And I get it. That's a terrible feeling—and a very real feeling. Credit card debt is a reality for millions of Americans.

I'm certain that when you got your first credit card, your intentions were to build your credit score, buy what you needed, and pay back your debt as soon as possible—until one day, it just wasn't possible.

Chances are, it's too late to plug the holes, stop the bleeding, and erase the debt with one or two payments. The determining event already happened, whether it was a missed paycheck, an extended illness that reduced your hours at work, or an unexpected emergency room visit with no insurance, and that event triggered a cascade effect.

Suddenly, you find yourself in the payment priority trap.

Let me explain.

Every consumer has just so much wallet share, so the money that comes in every month will be divided into expenses and other bills. When bills start adding up, you may think, W*hat's the least important payment I need to make?*

Wallet share fluctuates over time, and it changes with the economy. For example, from 2006 through 2008, the greatest payment priority and wallet share was housing and mortgage payments because housing values were skyrocketing. People perceived their house as an ATM, recognizing its value and making sure the mortgage was the first bill they paid every month.

When the bottom fell out of the housing market in October 2008, the payment priority we placed on our mortgages dropped significantly. Since our homes were then worth 30–40% of their previous value, we paid that bill *last* to be able to put food on the table and keep the lights on. Our collective uncertainty about the economy prompted us to make our credit card bills the number one priority, where they were historically the third or fourth highest priority.

So, in times of economic crisis, whether global or personal, people adjust their payment priorities based on the perceived importance or value of that specific bill. The desperate mindset is that there's nothing more a creditor can take. The phone calls are ignored, and the mail stacks up unopened in the middle of the dinner table. No one wants to answer the doorbell. No one wants to answer the phone. The blood pressure rises every time it rings.

I say, "Enough!"

Believe me; you're not alone in this. And the sooner you understand how you got to where you are, the sooner you can start making small steps in the right direction. And one of those important steps is making sure your mind is in line with your goals.

GETTING YOUR MINDSET RIGHT FOR THE JOURNEY AHEAD

While most of the advice available to those in debt crisis ranges from bankruptcy to budgeting, the harsh reality is that it is extremely hard for most people to budget. No one—especially me—wants to do the work to live within a certain reduced budget. You either have to earn more to pay off your debt or learn how to leverage the debt you have—bankruptcy being the nuclear option. Either way, it means you have to sacrifice to get through it.

Any way you slice it, a new mindset requires you to prioritize your debt. Start with your necessities, housing, utilities, food, and transportation, factoring in the variety of insurances that you'll need to operate your life. Those are fixed costs that should eat up anywhere from 80–85% of your entire wallet share every single month.

Everything left over is then directly related to your mindset. Do you spend the excess on erasing your debt, soothing yourself with unnecessary purchases, or impressing the people around you? Society has programmed you to believe your worth as a person is directly related to your assets, your credit score, and sometimes even about the specific credit card you've qualified for! *After all, why settle for a silver or gold card when you qualify for platinum?*

So, it's a constant battle between wanting a better lifestyle than you can afford and not being able to pay for more stuff. We've made credit cards a status symbol, the most marketed commodity out there behind sex, so it should come as no surprise that credit reporting agencies have preyed on this status hierarchy tied directly to your credit score.

It's not always the big-ticket items that set us back financially, and it's not the hundreds of thousands of dollars in hospital bills resulting from an out-of-the-blue accident. Most people fall into debt because of what I call "Death by a Thousand Cuts"—buying lattés and lunch every day instead of brewing coffee at home and brown-bagging it.

So many people who struggle with credit continue to make those choices because they are not operating on a finite set of capital resources; they're operating on seven revolving credit lines in their wallets. When one reaches its limit, there's another card to take its place.

But let me say it louder for those in the back, once and for all. Your worth as a person has nothing to do with how much debt you do or do not have or how well you manage your debt. While it's normal to feel upset or embarrassed about debt, *you do not have to feel that way*. In fact, the better you feel about yourself and your future in general, the more equipped you'll be to tackle your debt head on.

A little later on in this chapter, and with a deeper dive in chapter three, I'm going to teach you how to present your particular hardship in the best, most accurate light, from the bank's perspective. I want you to shift your mindset in so many ways, but we'll start with thinking like a bank.

HOW TO THINK LIKE A BANK REGARDING HARDSHIPS

Knowing that the bank's overall goal is to ensure that their credit card portfolio is performing at peak levels, they have built-in accounting procedures that they fall back on to reflect the true performance of that portfolio. Think about it for a minute. Since it's unrealistic to expect that 100% of people will always repay their debts, the banks must factor in a loss rate. Banks know that bad things happen to good people. They know they won't recoup 100% of their client's debt, but they expect to recoup a portion.

You need to understand where the bank is coming from. They are not looking to screw over good people. The banks want to lend money and be repaid in full. However, when you get into a debt situation, the bank has certain FDIC and OCC rules and guidelines they have to comply with. Therefore, their portfolio has to include an allowance for hardships.

There are varying degrees of hardship, the extreme being a terminal disease or a risk of self-harm or suicide, because the bank's probability of collecting on that person is next to nil. They might offer you a low settlement amount just to clear it up. (Disclaimer: The bank may also ask for proof or call the police to do a wellness check. Never lie about a terminal illness or thoughts of suicide to get out of a debt.)

On the other end of the spectrum, you have a temporary job loss, which is handled differently. Perhaps the bank will allow you to make a bare minimum payment on that account and re-age it back to *current* status if you're already delinquent. (We'll talk about the re-aging process later in chapter six.)

But for now, consider how the bank will measure your assets to recoup what is owed. Do you own a second home? Do you have a recreational vehicle? Do you have a boat? (No, you're not allowed to lie about your possessions. You can get yourself into major trouble that way.) They take that information concerning your assets and determine whether or not you have the ability to pay and a propensity to pay. And as for that propensity to pay, be aware that banks *may* coax you into compliance by using intimidation tactics and threatening to take those assets. However, there are laws to protect you from harsh collection tactics.

By analyzing your entire snapshot and teaching you how to shift your mindset toward doing whatever it takes to pay down your debt, we're going to find a way out of this together. Because the more you can begin to think like a bank, the easier it becomes to play their game and make progress toward your goal of becoming debt free. You'll see.

ACKNOWLEDGING AND ASSESSING YOUR SITUATION

To fully understand where you are financially and where you'd like to be, it's important to review your financial history and the circumstances surrounding your current situation. Once you fully understand how and why you have arrived at your current financial status, you can begin to create a plan to move forward.

You can find debt assessment tools and calculators online, or you can tally up your debt by reviewing all of your financial paperwork and accounts.

You can use our tools to do your own assessment.

A debt assessment is designed to quantify your debt and determine your options. Mental preparation is key to navigating the debt process because while it is often stressful, it's important to remember that debt is not in any way a reflection of your worth as a person, your value, and your abilities. It's simply a set of circumstances to navigate.

When it comes to personal finance, you need to know how much money you have coming in every month and how much is going out. What is your cash flow?

First, list all your current sources of income and *potential* sources of income. Can you pick up a second job? Do you have money coming in from a tax return or maybe an inheritance? Are there possessions you can liquidate?

Then you need to determine the types of debt that are involved. Make a list of every debt you have—anything you owe money on, past or present. Pull your credit report to find out where you stand. Again, your situation determines what options you have available to you.

Earlier, we touched on how you got here. Now, I want you to write down what circumstances led you to your current situation. Did you fall into one of the reasons people find themselves in debt that I mentioned earlier? Maybe it goes a little deeper than "I lost my job." I once had a client who lost her job due to discrimination. We were able to help her win a discrimination lawsuit that awarded her enough money to pay off all of her debt. Each person's situation can lead to different avenues of help.

The next step is acknowledging your situation in its entirety. When you look at your income and your debt side by side, can you muster the discipline to cut back on unnecessary daily expenses to start chipping away at the debt on your own? And will it be enough to start chipping away at your debt on your own? Or do you need to take a more drastic approach? Either way, dealing with your creditors is something you often can't get around.

YOUR LOAN HEALTH: A PERSONAL ASSESSMENT[1]

Regardless of the level of your debt, it is critically important that you fully assess your situation and know your capabilities and limitations. Here's how to take a temperature check:

- Verify the loans you have and the specific details, such as interest rate, amount owed, and the type of loan.

---

[1] Original section material provided by Larry R. Taylor, PhD. A personal debt assessment specific to student loans is available in chapter eleven, but this loan assessment can apply to anyone with any type of debt.

o What is the payment?

o Does the payment change during the life of the [loan]?

o What is your interest rate?

o What are the fees if you are late or miss a payment. What are the processes if you run into a financial challenge?

To keep on top of your debt and finances, do this type of assessment at least annually. Remember to document the date you did the review, so you don't let too much time lapse between assessments.

- The next part of the assessment involves determining the effect this debt payment may have on your monthly budget. Keeping in mind that these payments can go on for potentially dozens of years into the future, how is it affecting decisions surrounding you or your family's specific goals?
- Look for some indication of how your loans affect your level of stress, anxiety, and worry.

o Are you struggling to make payments?

o Do you frequently make late payments?

o Are you presently behind with payments?

o If you are behind, how many have you missed?

o Are you receiving calls about this debt?

The answers to those questions will give you an indication of the degree of the problem you have and will lead to the following considerations.

- Do you want to do some or most of the work yourself, or would you rather turn it over to someone else to help?
- Can you avoid letting the process get you down? Can you stay motivated to follow through?
- Are you willing to do the necessary homework to complete the job?
- Can you be disciplined about talking to collectors or loan servicers, working the details?

Gathering these details will save time, but they can also save you an incredible amount of money, heartache, and anxiety once you fully understand your financial picture and your comfort level in handling the debt yourself or by seeking help.

ACCEPTING THE COLD HARD TRUTH: YOU WILL HAVE TO DEAL WITH YOUR CREDITORS

Let's talk about one of the most difficult parts of this process; you will have to deal with your creditors, which means you must prepare and strengthen your mindset and set reasonable expectations for what's to come.

There are a host of emotions you'll experience if you've gone delinquent on your bills or are facing that inevitability, from shame and guilt to panic. Acknowledge them, and then let them go.

As I mentioned, your creditors will thrive on those feelings and use them against you. That's literally their job. They'll start with gentle reminder calls, and you'll likely feel compelled to tell the person on the other end of the line all the reasons why you've been unable to pay your bill. Unfortunately, that person may not have the authority to offer you any relief, but you'll still tell your story, and you'll continue to tell it to anyone who will listen. Everyone does it.

My only warning is that your *hardship story* has to stay the same throughout the process. Creditors can view your credit report, which includes all the credit lines you're paying as well as the ones you aren't, and one creditor may add information to your report about the hardship you've asserted to be true. Depending on that hardship, there may be options and programs available from the creditor to ease your burden, like an early charge-off program or settlement. But if you give a *different story* for why you're unable to pay every time someone calls, it won't add up in the notes section, they won't believe you, and they'll be less likely to try to work with you on options for settlement.

Your specific circumstance determines how you will deal with each creditor. If you decide to settle your debt, you might sign up with a company to help you. If you can make payments if the creditors lower your interest rate, you can continue to make more than the minimum payment and pay off the balance on your own. No matter what the situation is, knowing what your goal is and what the creditors' goals are will help you decide the direction you will take.

UNDERSTANDING YOUR HARDSHIP AND CREATING YOUR GAME PLAN

The credit card companies created this game, and we've all happily played along without paying attention to the score. But to win, you've got to decide on your game plan—it's either budget and sacrifice or understand the damage you're about to create for the next few months or even years. Either way, you're going to get through it and build your future from there. It really will be okay in the end.

It's crucial to lean into your decision once you have assessed your situation, whether you choose the avalanche method of prioritizing your debt with the highest interest rates, the Dave Ramsey snowball method of paying off your smaller debts first, or other options that might be much harsher.

Of course, the avalanche approach is the most effective number-wise, but the snowball method offers more opportunities for positive reinforcement and sets up an environment of wins, however small, that often do create a slow but steady result. We'll discuss this in depth later. However, for those whose situation is more dire, we will discuss the harder choices, such as credit counseling, debt management, debt settlement, or, worst-case scenario, bankruptcy.

As someone who has experienced credit wealth and a long-term cash lifestyle, I assure you that a positive and focused mindset is everything. It will connect you to your plan, keep you laser-focused on your spending, help you overcome the feelings of fear, desperation, frustration, and exhaustion you'll inevitably experience, and drive you toward success.

For now, I want to emphasize that your decision, whatever it is, *will* overwhelm you for a while, but it's crucial to wrap your mind around the plan you've chosen and why and then follow that plan until it works because it *will* work.

Next, we'll talk through the process of consumer debt. Becoming educated about the history of credit and how it works will set you up for success.

WHAT YOU CAN DO RIGHT NOW

- Mindset is key! If you are holding onto any guilt, remorse, or negative views of yourself for having debt, it's time to let that go. Debt does not in any way make you a bad person.
- Take this opportunity to do a little introspection. The more open you are to understanding and acknowledging your current financial situation, the easier it will be to make smart decisions.
- Get your game face on! Make a list of all the reasons you now find yourself in debt. Avoid any personal judgments or blame—this is simply an exercise you'll use later in chapter three to write out your hardship story.

CHAPTER TWO

AN OVERVIEW OF THE CONSUMER DEBT PROCESS

Credit has *always* been a reputation game. Someone keeps score, and there's a clear winner and a definite loser. But here's the kicker; the game never ends. Even more troubling, one side never has possession of all the rules in this game.

A few hundred years ago, merchants kept ledgers of payors who didn't follow through on their debts. They shared that information with each other, warning who in the community to avoid lending to. At a time when credit IOUs presumed the old adage, "My word is my bond," a reputation became instantly worthless upon unpaid debts.

It has always been a costly game.

THE HISTORY OF CREDIT

TransUnion was initially established as a holding company for a railway company called Union Tank Car Company based in Chicago, Illinois. A year after its inception, TransUnion bought the Credit Bureau of Cook County, and the rest is history. Bureaus back then were regional and helped a community keep tabs on its members. But when TransUnion entered the game, they turned local reporting into a national record. Experian, the newest on the block, started in 1996 as a multinational consumer credit reporting company. Since then, they've expanded their reach, selling decision analytics and marketing tools to businesses, as well as individual fingerprinting and targeting to protect consumers from fraud and identity theft. They are considered the most tech-advanced of the Big Three credit reporting agencies.

American Express started in the freight business and then introduced travel services like money orders in 1882 and traveler's checks in 1891. In those days, it was dangerous to take cash on international trips. But American Express protected travelers' money with an insured option that would be protected against loss or theft and could be exchanged at the going rate in any country. They opened their first Paris office in 1895, expanded to England in 1896, and Germany in 1898.

The game had gone global.

Diners Club was the very first credit card and was used exclusively in restaurants. According to lore, Frank McNamara forgot his wallet at a New York City restaurant and couldn't pay his tab. In 1950, just one year later, he showed up at another restaurant with a small cardboard card and used it in place of cash. Soon after, Visa and Mastercard created what they called payment rails—a system that moved money from payer to payee, connecting banks to businesses and individuals.

Credit card companies continue to be the ones making the rules and changing them to keep their advantage. As an informed consumer, you need to understand the current rules with the understanding that they will always continue to change—and always in favor of the credit card companies. How will they adapt to consumers understanding—and anticipating—those rules and changing their own strategies?

Game on.

IN THE GAME OF CREDIT, KNOWING YOUR OPPONENT IS KEY

Credit cards are one of the most widely marketed financial products in the world. In our high-speed, mobile app lifestyles, we all need at least one. Or we think we do.

It's the interest that ends the game for most of us. Think about how the interest is calculated and compounded on this type of credit vehicle. Credit card debt is an unsecured loan, which means its interest rates are astronomically high because the credit card companies don't require any sort of collateral to back the loan. When you buy a car or a house, that's a secured loan with some set collateralized asset guaranteeing the repayment of that loan or some portion of the repayment of that loan. On a $100,000 loan, for example, you may pledge $50,000 collateral.

But a credit card is an open-ended line of credit with no defined term of payoff and no specified amount.

"Charge what you want," it coaxes us. "Pay it back when you can. And, hey. We know we gave you a credit limit, but you can exceed it. We're here for you."

Even worse, credit card loans are a revolving line of credit, which means you can pay all of the charges or just some of the charges *at your discretion* every month. Those auto and home loans mentioned earlier are closed-end notes with a much more defined structure. Let's say the bank gives you $10,000 to buy that car, and, in return, you are expected to make payments on the fifth day of every month at a fixed interest rate of 3.8%. It sounds like a great deal until you do the math and realize you're getting screwed.

At some point in our lives, we were offered a store card that we could use to build points and earn rewards. Why would we ever say no to rewards? And why would we ever say no to building up our credit reputation? So, we say yes to the store card, then yes to another, and yes when they offer to increase our credit even more.

We are simply playing the game. But how well do you know your opponent?

The relationship between you and your creditor is like any other successful—or toxic—relationship. From the outset, it's key to know your role and responsibilities and familiarize yourself with theirs. Ask yourself about your creditors' intentions, and be very clear about your own, too. If you don't understand how or why you got involved in the relationship and who exactly is running the game, you will be at a severe disadvantage when problems arise.

At any given time in America, seventy-seven million people have at least one account in collections. They panic and don't know where to turn, so they run to a credit counseling company or a debt settlement company without knowing the next play. They assume there will be fees, but they also assume the promised services will be worth it. Most of the time, those promises are unfulfilled.

The rule to remember is that credit card companies expect to win the game—every single one. They will punish you whether you have a debt settlement or credit counseling company involved or not. They will hammer you with the rules you never knew were in play, and you will lose.

You will lose *unless* you learn the rules and study your opponent. It's about time we level the playing field, don't you think? Let me give you a peek behind the curtain, translate the tough talk, and provide some realistic plays to give you a fighting chance.

WHAT YOUR CREDIT SCORE MEANS AND HOW IT IS FIGURED

If you're squeamish, skip the next few lines. If you want to do what it takes to get out of credit debt hell, read on.

Credit is often likened to an open sore. It is always healing. And even when it recovers, there still may be a scar.

Credit is rarely perfect, yet approximately one-third of the population believes they have a perfect credit score, generally around 850, but anything above 720 is considered excellent. They've checked it for themselves on Credit Karma, so they feel more than qualified to buy a home or a car. They don't realize there are different types of credit scores: one that applies to car purchases, another one for mortgages, and one to get a credit card. They're all different.

My credit is 730, you might think. *I'm going to buy a house.*

The mortgage company has a different score. "Your credit is at 690." That changes the game entirely.

Depending on the feed used by your bank or mortgage company, it will likely differ from the averages of the three bureaus used by Credit Karma, Free Credit Score, or one of the other credit services. So, it's important to know all the numbers that figure into your credit score.

"But I'm afraid to look," you wince.

You're not alone. There have been times when I've been anxious about my credit score. I knew it was good, but what if it wasn't as good as I thought it was?

It's not only uncertain scores that worry us. I have friends who try and try to obtain a perfect credit score of 850 until it consumes them. Once they achieve it, I always ask, "Now what?"

The majority of the time, they're afraid to do anything to jeopardize that 850. And it's that hesitation that gives the credit companies the advantage. Consider it part of the intimidation tactics in the game of credit.

CREDIT CAN HEAL OVER TIME

A FICO score is the result of all the information in your credit history. It determines the deal your lender will make, from the amount you can borrow, the length of time to repay it, and the interest rates.

It's important, for sure. Yet, no one knows exactly how it's figured. The algorithm is proprietary, so it's not disclosed to anyone.

Here's what you need to know, though. It is entirely possible and easier than you would think to heal your credit score.

Read that again.

In a court case back in 2007, the Federal Trade Commission called an expert witness from TransUnion to testify about FICO. He elaborated on certain topics but not others, claiming that he was not at liberty to disclose the proprietary information. While he was on the stand, he testified that credit gets dinged along the way and then it charges off, and then it starts to heal again.

The judge stopped him for clarification. "Wait a minute. If I don't pay my debt again, and it charges off, my credit will get better anyway?"

The man answered, "Yes, your Honor."

"Does everyone know this?" the judge asked, clearly incredulous.

"No," the man laughed. "And let's keep it to ourselves."

Imagine all the secrets about credit that we don't know. It would level the playing field, wouldn't it?

But as it stands, anything to do with credit is so ambiguous. There is a perfect ratio of utilization on your credit card and so many variations that no one can say with any certainty, "If you do this, then this will happen."

If you have a $10,000 limit, some algorithms say the optimum ratio to enhance your credit score is to have $3,000 worth of utilization with a $7,000 available credit line. Unfortunately, no consumer knows that because FICO is only providing that information to the creditors.

But here's what I do know. Your credit score can heal. Seven years is the full cycle, but my credit went from zero to 700 in one year, with my only deficit being the age of my debt. Specifically, I hadn't had debt long enough. So, if you think you had bad credit, it could be worse; you may have *no credit score*.

I've helped so many people establish credit, and one of the easiest ways to do it is to get a few secured credit cards that can be paid off every time there's a charge. You can obtain the secured cards and pay them every week. Every *week*, not every month. It is the number of times you make a payment on your debt that drives up your score, which can jump from 450 to 650 within ninety days.

The important thing to ask yourself is, "What am I going to do with credit? How can it work for me?"

There are ways to optimize your credit score, from disputing accuracies to managing the exact balance-to-payment ratio. Depending on the creditor, there are certain times of the month when they update and report. Knowing those time frames and adjusting payments accordingly will optimize the updates on your bureau report. There are also favorable times to make big purchases based on when your potential creditor will run your credit report.

Understanding the different types of debt will help you think more like the bank, and you'll begin to make more educated choices about purchases.

TYPES OF ACTIVE AND PASSIVE DEBT

There are different asset classes of debt and different reasons people find themselves saddled with debt. Let's talk about active and passive debt.

Active debt is credit card debt. You had to physically take action or make a conscious decision to sign up and then use that card. It's the same for student loans, auto loans, and mortgages.

Passive debt is owed after an unforeseen event that's out of your control, like a medical expense. No one is extending you a line of credit to have a heart valve transplant. Unless you have life insurance that pays for final arrangements, a death in your family will result in signing up for some kind of credit line to help you pay. In medical cases, there's usually no time for any other option.

Medical debt is still reported to credit bureaus, but there is continued discussion about ceasing that sort of reporting because it is not debt consumers willingly sought. It's not called a *debt report*. So, if it's a credit report, then it should only include your record with credit. Credit reports should measure how you manage credit, and medical debt isn't credit.

More examples of passive debt occur when your car is towed or you have an outstanding traffic violation, which are either directly or indirectly reported to credit bureaus.

Is that fair? Or is it just another part of the game? And if it's a game, how can we get the upper hand?

We can break free of the debt cycle by understanding the differences in how the credit industry wants us to think and behave (become an avid consumer with multiple types of debt) and how we should be thinking and behaving if we want to get out of debt and remain debt-free.

As consumers, we're told to have a good mixture of different types of credit and a long credit history. So, what do we do? We rationalize that we should buy a new car to build or improve our credit.

After three years with a car, we get antsy and want a new one. It's still a reliable car, but we want that fresh car smell. We want that dopamine rush that comes when we drive away from the dealership in a brand-new model.

"I'm paying $525 a month on this car," you tell the dealer.

"No problem," they smile. "I can put you in a brand-new car, and your payment will only increase by $28 a month."

"An eighty-four-month loan should result in an eighty-four-month credit history, which will help raise my credit score, right?"

Right.

But in the meantime, the value of that new car instantly depreciates 25%. Worse, when you trade the car at the end of that eighty-four-month loan, you'll probably roll the remaining amount of that debt into a *new* car loan, which will likely increase the price well over what the original purchase price of the new car would have been. When you drive a new car off the lot, you will not only lose the 25% depreciation, but you will also bring in a negative balance from the prior loan. Double whammy!

Does that sound like a game you can win?

It's time to shift our entire thought process about credit and stop rationalizing active debt. Start with this. We're driving a payment, not a car.

A WELL-ROUNDED PERSPECTIVE ON THE DEBT DYNAMIC

The debt dynamic starts with applying for a credit card, transacting, possibly defaulting, getting into the collection cycle, fixing your credit, and starting over again. There are a handful of people who have experienced all sides of the debt dynamic, and I'm one of them. I've been extremely wealthy, and I've lost it all. I've had a credit score of zero and brought it back to its lofty heights. I've been a debt settler, a debt buyer, and most importantly, a consumer, just like you.

Years after I filed for bankruptcy and finally paid off the debt I had incurred from my previous relationship, my credit was shot, and I refused to get a personal credit card. Ten years later, I asked a friend to check my credit score out of curiosity, and he informed me that I didn't have one.

"It's that low?" I asked for clarification, a little shocked.

"No," he answered, slightly amused. "You have no credit profile, as in not even a zero credit score."

I decided it was time to get back into the credit game. I wanted to start buying real estate, and that meant building my credit. Because of my nonexistent credit score, I was forced to get a secured card, meaning I first gave the bank money, and they held it in a separate account, similar to a savings account, except there's no interest to collect. If you want a $2,000 credit limit, you give them $2,000 to hold in case you default. You simply use the card and make payments, and they report it to your credit bureau.

It took me three or four months to bring my credit score from zero to the 600s. By six months, it was well over 700. The funny thing is that in 2020, I bought nine properties in Los Angeles, California, and refinanced them for their equity with no problem. But when we tried to refinance *our* home in California to take advantage of a lower interest rate, my credit score was still too low for their program.

Imagine that.

But what about consumers who don't have a credit record and buy everything with cash? How do they factor into the credit industry?

THIN-FILE CLIENTS

"I don't even have a credit file."

Industry insiders call a certain segment of society thin-file clients—those with no history of servicing or paying back debt because they have never operated in a debt environment. The credit reporting agencies don't have information on those consumers, so they can't rate them as a credit risk.

Others who fall into that category are people who are unbanked or underbanked, which means they may have a bank account, but they don't write checks. Instead, they cash their checks at the bank and operate strictly off of cash, using money transfer services like PayPal to send money when necessary.

A company called eCredable determined that these thin-file clients have more of a credit history than the credit community originally believed. So, they set about building a picture of that payment history so creditors could determine their creditworthiness.

Again, they're not doing it out of the goodness of their heart. The impact of a cash customer on a bank is that their account offers the bank no benefits, as the bank doesn't have the deposits from which to lend against. They're not alone. Credit card companies lose out on money on merchant interchange fees and interest charges. Billions of dollars a year go across borders in money transfers, and, quite frankly, the federal government loses out on tax money for that purpose.

eCredable developed a reliability score for the former thin-file clients. Their algorithm and scoring models were accepted by Experian, FICO, and some of the other big credit reporting agencies. Eventually, Experian cut a deal with eCredable and white-labeled their product.

What is their goal? The goal is to make a segment of the population—historically off-the-radar of lenders because they couldn't sufficiently underwrite their credit risk—appear to be more credit-worthy by using alternative data. By doing so, lenders will be able to originate new lines of credit, adding more credit card users, personal and auto loans, and even mortgages.

Who are you betting on to win this game?

THE SYSTEM IS RIGGED AGAINST YOU

If you fall into debt, it's not all your fault. Those creditors have been watching you from the beginning, preying on you, issuing you more and more credit, inviting you deeper into debt. They make you feel like it's a natural state, a normal predicament that occurs when you live a normal life.

But they've set up a system where there's no easy way to get out of debt.

When you make that monthly payment, you believe that you are paying down your debt's principal and interest accordingly. However, what you don't know is that you're operating on a thirty-day billing cycle while the credit card company is on a fifty-five-day billing cycle, at a minimum. You can dig yourself out of that hole, but it will take time and effort.

No matter what online site you consult for help, they all have a credit card minimum payment calculator to make you feel more confident that they can help you pay off your debt. But they don't correctly calculate how interest rates are calculated on a credit card.

Here's how it works. On any credit card billing cycle, there is a current balance plus the new charges. The daily periodic interest rate, which is the annual percentage rate divided by 365, is then applied to the balance plus the new charges *on a daily basis*. Essentially, you have a new debt balance at the end of every day. At the end of the cycle for the next day, the daily periodic interest rate is applied to that new balance. Every day, a little bit of interest gets added to the balance, which means you are being charged interest on top of interest.

In a simple interest calculation, take the average daily balance for the billing cycle and multiply it by one-twelfth of the interest rate.

You can find an interest calculator here:

With credit card interest, if you start day one with a thirty-day billing cycle, you are adding interest every day during those thirty days. Then, your statement closes. When your statement closes, you have twenty-five days to pay your bill from the closing date. The credit card company has to give you that long to pay your bill, and they're happy to do it. Why? Because, in the interim, between the time your statement closes and the time your bill is due, they will continue to charge you interest every day of those twenty-five days. The only exception occurs when the full balance is paid, and there is no residual balance; all of the interest accrued between the closing statement date and time of the payment due date is reversed out, and the only debt owed is the closing statement balance. But if there's one penny of unpaid balance out there, you are going to accrue an additional twenty-five days of interest before that payment gets applied to your account.

That is the fifty-five-day billing cycle.

Even if you mistakenly believe you've paid off your credit debt, there may be an insignificant charge remaining on your balance. When it goes delinquent, you'll get a ding on your credit. Be prepared. There are mental games at play when we deal with debt.

You may feel guilty, and your creditors will do their best to make you feel like a deadbeat for not paying what you owe. However, it's important to remember all the years you've had a good relationship with the credit card company, and they made money off you, and you received the benefit of using their card and their credit. Now, circumstances beyond your control have changed the relationship.

It was mutually beneficial until it wasn't.

Debt relief options aren't one-size-fits-all, though. There are scenarios where someone opened a credit card and maxed it out right away, which gives the perception that the consumer is deliberately trying to game the system, and that puts them in a different category than someone who has had a card for ten years and is continually paying it off. Other factors that could come into play include salary or even your state of residence and how long the account has been active.

If you owe $2,500 at an interest rate of 17%, your credit card company requires a minimum payment. If followed, and you never make any more than the minimum payment, the payment schedule results in a total of $4,600 in interest charges, bringing the total owed to over $7,000.

Again, does any of this sound fair?

HOW CREDIT REPORTS WORK

"I want to check my credit, but I heard it deducts major points from my score."

Nope. Everyone is entitled to receive one free credit report every year. TransUnion and Experian both offer them, as do certain banks. Beyond that, your credit score won't suffer a bit when you check it—even if you check it every month.

There are all kinds of different credit report pulls. The most common is a soft pull when a creditor wants to offer you a store card or needs to make sure you qualify or if your employer or landlord runs a credit check.

If you've ever applied for credit at a store or online, you're on the radar. They start by targeting a region, and they target people ages nineteen to twenty-six who have a college degree and live in those particular zip codes. Your name pops up, and they send you an offer, which you accept. Then, you've got another tradeline reporting on your credit, and that is where the buildup begins; you've got the easiest possible credit to obtain, you show history and eventually work your way up to that American Express level of credit.

Those soft credit report pulls are solely for marketing purposes. They have no impact on your credit.

Then, there are hard inquiries that hit when purchasing a car or mortgaging a house. Those actions set off an alarm on your credit report and deduct points immediately. From that point, most bureaus won't continue to ding your credit score for a set period of time, so creditors can check your scores as many times as necessary while you shop for said home or car.

A hard inquiry for a mortgage dings your credit a little bit harder than an inquiry for a car purchase.

If you want to focus on more proactive ways to maintain a credit score, it's critical to keep your payment history impeccable, balance your credit utilization ratio, and possess a healthy credit mix, from credit cards to auto and personal loans and home mortgages. Just as importantly, keep a watchful eye on errors or fraud in your credit report and address them immediately.

CREDIT IS A STATUS SYMBOL

Wealth is a status symbol. If you're just starting, however, you usually don't have assets that garner attention. But having a big credit line is as close as you can get.

The right card speaks for you. Imagine paying a bill with the American Express Centurion Card, also known as the Amex Black Card. It's reportedly only available to those who spend over $100,000 a year, and there's an annual fee. Rewards are a draw to credit users, too. The Capital One Venture Rewards Card offers travel and spending incentives, while the Platinum Card from American Express gives access to over 1,000 airport lounges around the world. We justify that those perks are worth the steep annual fees. Perception is everything when it comes to reputation.

Here's the problem with credit; it's like the chicken and the egg. You want to buy a house, but you have no credit. So, you set out to establish that credit and prove that you're a trustworthy debt risk. In a perfect scenario, you would keep your credit under control, keep your debt-to-income ratio normal, and never miss a payment. You would obtain that optimum credit score and save money for a down payment. That is the ideal scenario.

But how many people follow that path? I don't know many.

If you play the game right, you can actually use credit cards to your advantage. For instance, if you had a big enough credit line on your card, you could use that as a cash advance and buy a house. If you bought a rental property with that cash advance, you could turn bad debt into good debt. There are so many different scenarios to win the game. You just need a little—or a lot—of risk tolerance.

THE BENEFITS OF CREDIT CARDS

Credit cards aren't the enemy. Nope. It's the allure and vague promises delivered by great marketing.

In a perfect world, you signed up for the credit card to establish credit and, as a welcome bonus, earn travel miles. And if you follow the rules and pay off your debt every month, that's exactly how the story goes.

It turns into a horror story only when we're not honest with ourselves. Most people use the carrot of the miles to justify their charges on the card and getting into debt. The excuse is, "It's fine! I'm earning points!"

But what if I told you that it takes $25,000 of purchases to buy a $180 plane ticket? "Oh my gosh," you'd say. "That's ridiculous. It's cheaper to buy a plane ticket outright!"

And what if I told you everything that we think we know about credit is wrong?

What if I told you there was a better way to play this game?

What if I told you this is a game, one that you can win—an extremely advanced marketing and publicity game to get people to purchase things they don't need?

WHAT YOU CAN DO RIGHT NOW

- Understand that credit is a game, and your FICO score can heal over time. Whew!
- Begin to shift your perspective about using credit (both the specific type of card and what that credit can buy) as a status symbol. If you don't need it, don't buy it or be guilted into a purchase because *everyone else is doing it*.

CHAPTER THREE

INSIDER SECRETS

If a picture paints a thousand words, a credit report tattoos a never-ending story on your entire body and follows you wherever you go.

That's a bit harsh, but it's the truth.

We're brainwashed. Our self-worth is tied to our credit score, meaning the amount of debt we carry related to our assets and payment histories tells everyone what they need to know about us. We're good. We're excellent. We're somewhere in between fair and poor. Forget about the ones who fall into the very poor designation. They're worthless. But actually, you're not.

CREDIT IS A TRAP

From the moment you opened your first credit card, you popped up on the credit bureau's radar, and they began tracking your every movement. What will your path tell them?

Maybe they'll see that your monthly payments are made on time with extra added to pay off your balance quickly. Or maybe they'll see the warning signs.

But you're not worried. In your mind, you've got it under control. Better yet, you feel fantastic when you go out and buy dinner or those expensive shoes. That credit card makes you feel like someone.

The next card is offered to you, and it feels like you've reached a new level of worthiness. The credit card company believes in you. They know how well you manage your money. They understand that you're someone.

Meanwhile, the credit bureau is still watching. They're the first to know when you apply for that American Express Platinum and the first to know when you reach your limit on it.

Before you know it, you're overextended and don't know how you're going to pay back all the money you owe. The only ones who aren't surprised by this development are the credit bureau and your credit card companies. This is their game, after all, and you've played it just as they hoped. They've marketed their cards using colors and precious metal descriptors, even constructing the card out of carbon fiber or stainless steel to make them even more covetable. And it works.

Wait until my friends and family see me pay with this card, you think.

You feel free and powerful as if you actually have money. College students who exist on ramen and peanut butter forget their student loans and say things like, "Drinks are on me!" Entry-level associates want to dress like the C-suite executives and shop accordingly. Perception is everything.

At no point in your thought process, however, is one thought of how you will pay for your charges. That is the power of credit cards; they make us forget reality and imagine the possibilities.

But I'm earning points, you may be thinking.

Yes, credit card companies love offering perks to their users because they help them rationalize their irresponsible activity. But if we stop and do the math, we know that those miles never add up the way we think they will.

In our mind, we're charging to earn a Hawaiian beach vacation. But if we do the math on what it will take to earn a round-trip ticket to Hawaii, it's going to take approximately $50,000 in spending to secure a $500 round-trip coach, back-of-the-bus, sitting next to the lavatory seat on a carrier, assuming that you can even find a seat that isn't sold out a year in advance based on reward miles. The outrageous revenue airlines earn just from the sale of miles to credit card companies will soon exceed the revenue generated by flying passengers on routes in the U.S.

Your points are pointless.

It's not just about status. Credit cards hold power over our lives and make them easier. With one swipe, we can fill up our gas tanks to get to work, pay our hairdresser, and order from Amazon. We prioritize them over other bills—even our mortgages.

It's interesting to look at our payment priorities. There are several studies on categorizing the different expenses in our lives and the order in which we pay them every month. It changes based on the perceived value of each expenditure.

Credit cards are always at the top of the list.

We protect our credit cards because we need them to buy a plane ticket for work travel, get a hotel room, grab a rental car, and take a client to dinner. If we get a flat on the way to our job, we need that credit card to buy new tires. We can't risk being without one.

Every credit card company has twenty-seven variants of a credit card for the sole purpose of moving you into a new card product every time you need more credit.

Data doesn't lie. Your creditors can predict your spending patterns before you finish ordering your first $7 latté of the morning. They know when you've reached your limits, when you need an increase, and when to offer you another card. There seems to be a solution around every corner with your creditors, usually in the form of another line of credit. So, you continue to spend that invisible money without consciously connecting to the amounts.

"Transfer your balance to our card," they offer. "Zero interest for nine months!"

You say yes to that one and promise to pay off your balance in nine months.

"No new charges," you vow. "I'll only use it for emergencies."

At that point, every charge is an emergency.

What does that tell you about the game? Even if we don't want to be on the team, we still have to play.

PERKS AREN'T PERKS

You will never beat the credit card companies and win the cash-back or frequent-flyer-mile game. They are laughing all the way to the bank. In exchange for your free ticket to Hawaii, the credit card company received all the interchange fees on every dollar you spent. Then, every time you didn't pay a balance, they got the daily accruing interest on that outstanding balance in the form of interest added to the account. In essence, you are paying for your perks time and time again.

The perks are just one way credit card companies differentiate their value from the competition to persuade you to choose their card, and then they want you to use their card. They don't make money if you're not charging transactions to their card. If you only use it twice a month and pay your bill in full, they're losing money on you because it costs them money to service the account to keep it active and to send you a statement.

And they want those interchange fees, or the fee the credit card company charges to move the transaction down the rails of the credit card system.

But that's not the only way they make money from your charges. There's also a merchant fee, which is the fee that the merchant—the grocery store, the restaurant, the gas station—pays to the credit card company. We can't forget about interest and annual fees, either. Yes, people pay for the privilege of using a status card, rationalizing it based on the perks.

Assess those perks realistically because the benefits can offset your fee if you actually use them. For instance, the American Express Platinum Card carries a $600 annual fee. If you use it on a flight with United Airlines to buy food or alcohol or a movie in flight, American Express will credit you back up to $200 a year of those charges. Then, there are other categories, like two $50 Uber credits a year, which adds another $100 coming back.

Remember, they're not extending those perks out of the goodness of their heart. They benefit from the perks even more than you do. By ensuring you'll use their card to reap the supposed benefits and by exposing you to different opportunities to use their card, their ultimate goal is to get you to change your habit of using one payment method and use their credit card instead.

There are credit card companies that ask their users to sign up every month to opt into the savings categories for that particular month. By physically performing an action on their website and essentially clicking the spending categories they've selected, they're leading us to spend targeted money.

"If you use your credit card this month to buy groceries," they generously offer. "we'll give you 5% cash back."

"Well," you rationalize. "That's a better deal than if I use my debit card, which is how I normally pay for my groceries. I'll do it this month."

If you buy $200 worth of groceries, that's $10 back. What they're counting on is that you won't pay off your balance every month, and the interest alone is more than the $10 you just saved.

Here's a way to benefit from the system. Charge all of your household expenses every month, like telephone, cable, gas, electricity, and water. If you never miss a payment, it will cost you the same amount as if you'd set up an auto-payment or written a check. At the end of the year, use your points to buy some airline tickets. That is the only way to win an unwinnable game.

Has anyone checked the score lately?

HOW THE COLLECTIONS PROCESS WORKS

It's not easy to deal with creditors, especially if you've let your debt go unpaid. There's no sympathy, no leniency, and no coddling.

If you've missed one payment, you'll receive a pleasant reminder call, gently inquiring whether you realize you've forgotten what day your payment was due. Eventually, they're threatening to contact your employer, garnish your wages, send you to collections, and possibly even take you to court.

Collections and recovery are broken down into pre-charge-off and post-charge-off. Anything prior to the account charging off is still considered collections because they haven't written your account off yet.

During that period, collections are broken down into thirty-day buckets (we'll discuss buckets in depth in chapter four). Collection tactics get progressively harsher as they get closer to charging off your account. Here's the nuance, though; the creditors are going to get harsher. However, the amount they are willing to settle for typically gets smaller as they realize the likelihood of repayment decreases.

Once the account is in post-charge-off, the bank has several options. They can choose to warehouse the debt (meaning they sit on it and wait to decide how to handle it), or they can send your account to a third-party collection agency, send it to a law firm to file suit to recover their monies or sell the debt for pennies on the dollar.

I want you to remember that almost everything in life is about negotiating—relationships, salaries, business meetings, and even household chores—and debt is no different.

No one tells you there's another way beyond paying in full or declaring bankruptcy.

If you're interested in settling your debt, it's time to strike a deal of sorts with your creditors.

HOW LENDERS LOOK AT YOU AND TREAT YOUR DEBT

From the beginning, lenders are looking at you as a potential asset. It's not personal to them; you are a number, and they are looking to see how much money can be made off of you. However, when they notice that there is a problem, they will start to handle your account based on the information they have collected, such as:

- History of your account
- Length of time being a client
- Your age
- Your health
- Your assets
- Employment
- Your propensity to pay
- Where you live
- Potential hardships

Striking a deal with you will depend on your specific circumstances and the type of debt owed. If you have no assets, no income, or a poor health condition, they may agree to a twenty to thirty cents on the dollar repayment plan. But if you've got assets, a steady income, and you've simply fallen behind on payment, they may be willing to accept a seventy-five to eighty cents on the dollar proposal.

Now we're evening out the score a bit.

THE TRUTH ABOUT LAWSUITS

Using algorithms and other data that's never been disclosed, the banks decide which debts are worthy of a lawsuit and which can be sold to a collection agency for pennies on the dollar. Some states are stricter than others; you may have the right amount of assets or they consider the length of time you've worked at your job. If they determine that the odds of recouping the debt are in their favor, they will sue.

Like I've explained, you may receive a gentle nudge the first month you miss a payment. The second month's communication is a little less gentle, and the third and fourth month messaging escalates accordingly as they recognize there's a problem. Between the fifth and sixth month of non-payment, just before the sixth-month charge-off, is the prime time to settle your debt before they send it to collections. They realize you've reached rock bottom, and they'd like to present an agreeable offer to collect something before they decide on your R9 charge-off. (An R9 is when a lender charges off a consumer's debt as a loss and inflicts the worst damage to a consumer's credit score at the six-month point of non-payment.)

When banks charge off an unpaid debt, they have to offset that loss with their reserves. It benefits them to try to settle the debt before they reach that point.

On average, it costs them about $500 just to file the lawsuit, so they will gauge whether or not your debt is worth that expense, asking themselves, "Are we throwing good money after bad?"

OLD DEBT NEVER REALLY DIES

Most people assume that the older the debt gets, the less it is worth.

I'm safe, you may be thinking. *It's been three years without a collections call. It's over!*

Not so fast. Remember when I told you that your credit history is tattooed on your body and that you're being tracked from the very moment you open your first credit card? It's the truth. And while you may assume that silence from your creditors is golden, debt collection is a long game.

No matter the age of your debt, assume your creditors are watching your every move—because they are. If you get a raise or move into a new home, or any other action pops up on your credit report, they'll show up and start the whole process over in an attempt to recoup the full balance.

"But there's got to be a statute of limitations," you say, hopefully. There is, and it varies from state to state. But that's not going to help you when the calls begin again.

You must remember that your unpaid debt stays on your credit report for seven years. Depending on your particular state statutes, your creditor has four years to legally collect on the debt, maybe more and maybe less. Beyond that time, they can still try to collect on it, but they can't *legally* collect on it.

That's right; they have no legal authority and can no longer sue you, but they can call and harass you. Worse, they can trick you into making a small payment, using coercion like, "Consider it a gesture of goodwill," and, "You don't want to be a deadbeat, do you?"

Do you know what happens after that payment? The clock resets, and another statute of limitations begins fresh. Get ready for many more years of those phone calls.

PARKING DEBT

Nothing in debt collections is black and white. I can't give you the exact roadmap to a settlement because there are so many variables and unscrupulous people on both sides.

Some illegitimate collection agencies will buy a portfolio of debt for fractions of pennies on the dollar and throw that on your credit report, even when it's not fully your debt. That is what is referred to as "parking debt." It is illegal, but it happens. It's one of the main reasons why I recommend checking your credit report often.

If anyone offers you credit repair to get false information off of your credit report, do your research on that company before you agree to use them. Credit repair businesses are viewed harshly by state and federal regulators, and a lot of people associate them with a scam. They send out computer-generated form letters and flood the bureaus with paper.

The bureaus got wise to their business practices and responded accordingly. If they suspect you've hired a credit repair company, they will advise you to get a refund and cease all correspondence with the company.

One thing credit repair companies do is ask the creditor to validate the debt to prove you owe that money. Validation could be personal information to validate the account is yours or the original signed contract with your signature. That is a beneficial tactic because, many times, the account begins with an original creditor or even a bill, which is sent to a third party for collection. Months or even years can pass before you get a bill from a doctor that you assumed was covered by insurance.

It's imperative to ask, "How do you know this is my debt? I require proof."

Until they provide that documentation, there are no more threatening calls. Further, you can also send your letter of dispute to the credit bureaus as an alert that it is not a valid debt, asking them to remove it from your credit report.

Of course, there are legitimate companies to use for credit restoration, so do your research.

You can find some we trust here:

HARDSHIP STORIES AREN'T HARD

We touched on your hardship story in chapter one, but here we'll go into more detail about the importance of a solid—and truthful—hardship scenario. Very few consumers realize that credit card companies have allowances for an entire checklist of hardships.

But first, how is hardship defined? A hardship is a legitimate disruption or displacement of your income. At the most basic level, it is an occurrence in your life that prohibits you from working.

Your creditors need to be aware of the specific hardships that are preventing you from paying your debt. If you're receiving Social Security or disability payments, it's important to document proof of your fixed income to collections to qualify for that hardship.

People often wonder if they can really settle their debt because of a hardship. The short answer is yes, sometimes.

I don't want to tell my creditors anything personal, you might be thinking. Negotiation doesn't make sense to you because creditors aren't openly offering that solution. But the FDIC and the OCC have made provisions for hardship situations that allow the credit card companies to settle on an amount less than the full balance.

Several qualifying hardships can impact your debt settlement, including illness or injury, taking leave from work to care for a sick relative, a change in employment status or a reduction in hours, medical bills, divorce, death, military deployment, and a fixed income situation for seniors, including compounded categories like seniors on a fixed income who are also suffering from a medical issue. But there is a whole range of other hardships that help with settlement options, suspending past due amounts, or lowering your minimum payments.

Interestingly, the fastest-growing demographic in credit card debt are individuals over seventy-two years of age as a result of their fixed and finite income. They receive a Social Security check and maybe even a pension check or some other type of retirement income, but they're not in the position to make additional money, and they're unable to pick up a second job. Even if they do, there's a trap for people in that category. As they start to make more money and move up in the tax bracket, the tax rate they end up paying on their total income is a higher rate, which reduces the net income they have in all their sources of income combined. So, even if they work more, they make less overall. That seems incredibly unfair, doesn't it?

Given our current financial environment, many creditors are backing off their entrenched stances around the settlement of debts. They realize everyone is under an undue amount of stress financially, but they also don't want to face additional loss reserves. Documented hardship cases don't affect the banks' loan loss reserves that they keep to offset their losses from things like credit card debt or bad loans.

It's important to realize that the statement, "I can't pay my bills," is not a hardship. Neither is "I owe more than I earn." But those excuses aren't the root of the problem for most of us.

What causes the problem is that people have maxed out their credit cards and have been making the minimum payments to service the debt for a long time. On paper, they're bankrupt. They're not putting any money into savings, and they don't have an emergency account. Then, there is that one event that takes them over the edge and starts the downward spiral.

It could be something as simple as an unexpected repair on your car or an appliance that dies in your kitchen. The extra charges increase your minimum payments, which you can't meet. You may be late with your payment one month and miss the next, which is a fifty-point hit on your credit score. From there, it's like a snowball rolling downhill. The credit card company moves your penalty rate from 17% to 29.99%, and pretty soon, that snowball is the size of a Mack truck, and it's heading your way, fast.

It's so subtle, most of us never see it coming.

Your hardship may come as a complete surprise to you, which will affect your reaction time. That's why it's imperative to have a savings account, an emergency fund, an attitude of action, and a plan ready to implement.

But most people don't do that. They come home shell-shocked. They pour themselves a cocktail, sit down on the couch, and feel sorry for themselves. They post their sob story on social media and respond to every comment. And it's a month before they remember all of the unnecessary subscription services and bills they won't be able to pay.

Wallowing in denial is a great way to lose the game, but it doesn't have to be that way. I'm not saying you won't experience a range of emotions with debt, but the longer you fail to act, the more ground you'll have to cover to get back on top.

So, get angry. Be sad. Be frustrated with your current circumstances. And then decide that you are going to do something about it, right now.

WHATEVER YOU DO, DON'T LIE

"Maybe if I tell them that I've lost everything, they'll forgive my loan."

Ethics and fraud aside, banks know when you're lying. They have access to your credit report, but they also use other services to gather information about you. They see that you have a second home, recreational vehicles, and a steady income. They know whether they can garnish your wages. They'll know when you're lying.

Now, credit card collections will have a bit more limited information. They won't know about family heirlooms, inheritances, or antique jewelry. But when you are in default, they know exactly how far they can push and how hard.

WILL YOU GET SUED?

In order of importance, most people in debt are worried about the damage to their credit score, whether or not they are going to be sued, and finally, creditor harassment.

It's not common knowledge, but creditors can't call you if you're represented by an attorney; by law, they must make all communication through your representation. Non-attorney companies don't have the same power of the legal process to stop creditor harassment.

Getting sued depends on many factors. Again, the creditor is looking at several reasons for you defaulting on your payments. One statistic shows that 11% of consumers who default on their debt are sued. It is expensive for the lenders to go down that road, so they are selective about who they file suit against.

If you are sued, don't panic. Nothing has changed; you still owe the same amount of money. It is just their way of getting your attention and using the legal process to collect the debt faster. It may also be an opportunity for you to present your case to the court if you have a legitimate reason for defaulting.

WHO GETS PAID FIRST?

It's not uncommon for someone in debt to have multiple creditors demanding repayment. So, who gets paid first?

A debt management program works well for a while because all of the creditors involved agree to a plan where they will be repaid 100% of their principal, and they will also be able to monitor payments as they are made. But not all creditors agree to that.

In a debt settlement program, the consumer and debt settlement company will determine who gets paid first depending on a variety of criteria merged with the bank's criteria. If a bank is playing hardball and they say they won't work with debt settlement, they will be last on the payee list. Conversely, if they're easy to work with, they are first on the list.

If you're delinquent on six credit lines, you may be fielding calls from six different agencies or banks multiple times a day. It gets overwhelming. Even if you enter a debt settlement program, they won't stop.

"I can't take any more phone calls!" you yell at your phone.

You can familiarize yourself with your state's laws related to creditors that can protect you. Banks have the most freedom legally to call than a third-party agency; a simple cease and desist letter should stop an agency's calls, and there is legal recourse if they violate federal laws. Chapter ten will cover this more in depth.

Know that you're going to receive a lot of phone calls. You don't have to answer them, but they will continue until your debt is addressed.

"They're threatening to show up at my house and take back my furniture!"

Even though they sound like they'll follow through on their threats, the odds are slim that they will come to your home to collect.

"Can they get a lien or garnish my wages?"

Not without your knowledge. If you're sued, you will be served legal documents laying out their complaint against you. As a general rule, out of the people who end up in collections, only a small percentage are getting sued, as mentioned earlier. Of the percentage who get sued, 90% receive a default judgment, meaning the consumer didn't show up in court to explain why they can't pay their debt.

Now, that is a missed opportunity. Cases like that are usually held in small claims court, where judges tend to be very lenient toward consumers and very harsh toward creditors. Some judges just throw cases out.

So, don't be afraid to fight!

THE HIERARCHY OF PAYBACK

Your biggest weapon in getting out of debt is your income. Admittedly, it also works against you because creditors know your income and your expenses, and they'll use those balances against you. Their goal is to be first in line for payback.

They are all trying to be first in line. The hierarchy of payback is determined by debt amounts, but the flexibility—or lack thereof—of the creditors contributes, too.

For example, let's presuppose that you owe Capital One $1,200 and you owe American Express $10,000. There will be a greater opportunity to settle on the Capital One balance first, as American Express might be a little stiffer.

Speaking of secrets that credit card companies don't want you to know, if you ever default on an American Express card, they have a policy stating they *will never issue you another card*. They have programs on their premium cards where they'll demote you to a lower level as a penalty.

WHAT YOU CAN DO RIGHT NOW

- Understand that *perks* are just elaborate marketing schemes to get you to spend more money.
- Remember that list you made in chapter one about the reasons you're in debt? Use that list to begin writing out your hardship story. Read and revise it until you're comfortable saying it out loud because you'll need to be able to repeat the same story to the creditors and collectors.
- Check your credit to see if there are any items listed that you don't recognize. Make sure no one has "parked debt" on your account.

CHAPTER FOUR

CHOOSING YOUR PATHWAY FORWARD

In the previous chapter, I gave you a behind-the-scenes peek at a few insider secrets that banks and creditors don't want you to know. We have also looked at the overall debt consumer process and the importance of having the right mindset.

Now that you are armed with that powerful knowledge, it's time to begin taking action. In this chapter, I want you to begin looking at your options and decide where to go from here. After all, you picked up this book to help get you out of a bad situation, right?

When I was a kid, some of the most popular books were from a series called *Choose Your Own Adventure*. Every chapter in each book gave you a choice at the end. A single book could contain an endless array of story possibilities.

The same is true for your financial life. There are endless possibilities, both good and bad. But don't let that stop you. All the knowledge in the world won't do you any good unless you commit to taking the next steps.

The first one involves learning to look at yourself in a whole new way.

LOOK AT YOURSELF THE WAY A CREDITOR DOES

When you look at your financial situation, there are naturally a lot of emotions involved. You may feel frustrated, guilty, ashamed, angry, or hopeless. Everyone who has tried to dig their way out of debt has felt those same things.

But as you embark on the journey toward a better financial future, I challenge you to look at yourself the way a creditor does.

What does that mean? It means looking at yourself as a business. *But I'm not a business; I'm an individual,* you may think. That's true. However, a creditor will look at you not as a person with hopes and dreams but as a legal entity with assets, liabilities, and income. A creditor doesn't look at your financial picture through the lens of emotion, memories, or personal potential. They see you only through the lens of numbers.

When you understand that this is how they see you, it's much easier to begin making headway because you see things from their point of view.

I have put together a tool to give you an overview of these three key elements of your financial health (assets, liabilities, and income):

This resource will help you gather enough information to help you know which pathway to choose as you move forward. It doesn't mean you are committed to that path. It is simply giving you information to help you make the best decision.

For example, you may choose to sacrifice your credit score for a while to get the debt load off your back. Or you may choose credit counseling because, in theory, it will do the least amount of damage to your credit.

As they say, *knowledge is power*. When you have more and better information, you can move forward with confidence. Let's look at a few different scenarios.

The first example is someone who would be considered "judgment proof." That means they don't have any assets, yet they have a lot of liabilities. Maybe their income is erratic, which usually means they haven't been at their job a long time. They don't have a house, yet they have a big car payment. These people work, move, work, and move. Rinse and repeat.

A creditor would see that and realize they have nothing to go after.

Of course, there are different grades of a "judgment-proof" individual. The bottom line is that if you are in that situation, there is nothing a creditor can get from you. You know you can go into a negotiation swinging a big stick.

A second example is someone with a lot of assets, very few liabilities, a steady income, and perhaps even passive income. Maybe they have been at their job for many years. That person is an easy target for creditors. They are analyzing the person's situation to see what they can get. If you are in that situation, you need to play differently than the person who has no assets because you're a different kind of target.

You have lots of personal choices along that spectrum. For example, someone may analyze their situation and think, *Credit counseling may be the solution for me. It's going to help me reduce my interest rate and lower my monthly payment. I am going to take a hit on my credit for a while, but I am going to pay back my creditors in full. At the end of the day, I am going to be clean.*

Likewise, another person may take this view. "I don't care. I just don't want to pay them anymore. I'm sick of it. I've been paying them for twenty years, and they have made a lot of money off me. I'm tired of this." Even though they know their situation makes them a big target, they are willing to take that risk.

Sometimes, the clear choice isn't necessarily the one people make. There are endless scenarios. When you combine that with all the emotions that come from financial stress, people sometimes make surprising choices.

Take some time to analyze your situation so you know where you stand. You can't make an informed decision until you have good information. Do you want to go down the safe path of debt relief, the slightly more aggressive path of credit counseling, or the even more aggressive approach of debt settlement?

Or is your situation so bad that you need the nuclear option, bankruptcy?

There are many possibilities. In the rest of this chapter, you'll discover some of the most important keys to help you make the best choice.

YOUR MINDSET IS THE MOST CRITICAL INGREDIENT OF YOUR SUCCESS

We have already taken a whole chapter earlier in the book to talk about mindset. Why bring it up again? Because without the right mindset, it's almost impossible to deal with creditors and come out victorious on the other side.

No matter which option you choose to settle your financial problems, it's going to take patience. It's going to take persistence. It's going to take resilience and strength. So, you've got to make sure your head is in the right space.

When people start to get distressed or are locked into habitual spending patterns and not paying attention to what is going on, they do so out of emotion. It's easy to get stuck in a mental pattern where you believe your means are greater than they are.

For example, take someone who makes $40,000 a year. They don't want to accept the fact that they are spending $80,000 a year. The same could be true for someone making ten times that amount. If someone makes $400,000 a year yet spends $800,000, they are no better off than the person with one-tenth of their income.

If your income is not very high, it's easy to believe that everyone who makes more than you is better off. Not true. Anyone who is spending beyond their means is living in the danger zone. All those people, no matter their income, are living in denial.

Everyone takes a hit at some point. We all deal with life circumstances that throw a wrench into our finances—an unexpected medical event, loss of a spouse, elimination of a job, a pandemic, or simply not being prepared for the inevitable crisis.

When we get into those situations, we generally lock up and become stressed. And when you feel stressed, you don't think clearly. You spend all your time and energy looking for the least painful way out of the situation.

Sound familiar? Don't feel bad. We've all been there.

People inherently do not like to take an introspective approach. Why? Because, quite frankly, we are afraid of what we will find.

When it comes to debt and finances, we find that we can't sustain what we are doing. However, we typically don't want to face that. So, things start to cascade pretty quickly. It might just be that we've been living "on the bubble," living paycheck to paycheck. Then an unexpected event happens, and now we have enough to pay all the bills except for one credit card. Then we say, "Well, I'll just let that one go this month and will catch up next month."

That begins the cycle of what we call "rolling buckets."

DELINQUENT CREDIT WORKS IN BUCKETS

You get thirty days behind on your payments, then sixty days. Pretty soon, you've got all the balls in the air, and you are juggling. All the while, you are trying to plug the hole by getting more money into the pipeline.

You don't usually start with getting an extra job and driving for Uber three nights a week to cover your mounting expenses. It starts with personal loans for people with bad credit or trying to find someone to give you money to help tide you over. Or maybe it is a payday loan or some other type of short-term solution. No matter how you slice it, you find out pretty quickly that you have just dug yourself a bigger hole. Now what?

Delinquent credit works in buckets. Imagine the first bucket is days 1 to 30. The next bucket is 60 to 90 days, then 90 to 120 days, 120 to 150, and the sixth bucket is days 150 to 180.

The collections process works the same way. Every month you're delinquent on a debt, it is a ding on your credit. At the end of that six months, the bank has to deem it a bad debt and charge it off. It's purely a financial maneuver. If the banks had their way, they would love to settle debts and negotiate repayment of at least part of the debt. But that's not necessary; they've already won the game.

Let me explain. When a bank issues a certain type of credit, it's called a portfolio. That portfolio contains a lot of people's money, so it isn't necessarily the bank's money that's at risk. It is hedge fund money. It is mutual fund money. It is pension fund money. And all those monies are invested in those portfolios.

The bank is the servicer of each of those portfolios. To show how that portfolio is performing at any given time, regulations are in place that dictate how that portfolio is treated. When debt occurs, there are very specific responses available for every situation and a clear set of guidelines of what the banks can and cannot do to handle that debt. Since debt dictates the performance of that portfolio, it must be regulated so the investors in that portfolio aren't misled in any way.

Here's the interesting part.

When the bank assembles a portfolio, they understand there will likely be a certain percentage of people who will not pay. For example, maybe they factor in a 5% default rate on the portfolio. In response, the banks insure their portfolios on that 5% default so they are covered if and when it occurs. The result is two separate revenue line items—one is the performance of that portfolio, meaning they are still receiving on-time payments on the debts, and the other is a revenue line on that 5% default. The bank has taken the loss on the default, but they are also insured against that loss, and they are still able to try and collect.

What does that mean for you as the consumer? The bank has gotten paid back twice. Still think the credit game is fair?

By now, you find yourself asking, "How do I get out of this mess?" One of the best ways to start moving forward is to use a process I call "Stop, Drop, and Budget."

STOP, DROP, AND BUDGET

When we were kids, our teachers taught us what to do if we were on fire—stop, drop, and roll. When your whole financial world is on fire, you've got to do something similar—stop, drop, and budget.

It means cutting off all expenses that are nonessential to your housing, healthcare, and food security. It includes subscriptions and automatic payments such as cable television, eating out, going to the movies, birthday gifts, and more.

I went through a time in my life when I didn't buy anyone a Christmas or birthday gift for five or six years. Why? Because I wasn't going to put $2,000 on a credit card to feel like I had to show someone I loved them by buying them a gift. When you're in that situation, you fight with the emotion of wondering what they will think of you. You imagine they will think you are a loser who is too broke to buy a gift, so you rationalize spending $50 to $100 on that person because you didn't want them to think badly of you.

But guess what? They will probably think poorly of you if you aren't taking care of yourself or your family and if you can't maintain your hygiene or feed your kids. Don't get to that point. Stop, drop, and budget.

As I mentioned, stop the automated payments. Don't give anyone access to your finances because that money disappears, and you don't even know where it goes. Drop anything nonessential. If it doesn't involve keeping your job, keeping food on the table, or keeping a roof over your head, you don't need it.

Here is the trick to doing it: You have to build a budget. You must find out where every penny goes every single month. Then, and only then, can you determine whether you make enough money to sustain the kind of lifestyle you are living.

We keep coming back to this question: How do you take an honest look at yourself to analyze your situation and see where you are today?

It's a painful process for most people. But when you face your problems head-on, you are much better equipped to deal with them. It starts with looking at how much money is coming in each month and how much you are spending. When I was younger, I used to joke that I had a $10,000 American Express bill, but it sure didn't feel like I had $10,000 worth of fun this month. When you start looking at what you got for your $10,000—that weekend trip to Vegas, fancy dinners, concert tickets, or buying gifts for your family and friends—you realize that it was all to impress someone else or for a fleeting moment of happiness. You are never getting that money back.

This whole process is designed to take an honest, very detailed look at yourself, which is painful. The bottom line is that you will never be successful in any program until you decide to take that next step.

Until you understand honestly where you are, accept your situation, and then decide to do something about it . . . you can't build a plan to go somewhere different.

If you don't know where you are, and you don't know how much you have to make up every month, you can never build a plan to get to that destination. If you live beyond your means, you must put together a strategy to live beneath your means. And how do you gamify that approach? Can you put together exercises, activities, or events where you try to spend the least money possible?

I always tell people, "When you get in your car and leave the house, you are going to spend $60 before you get home." Here is a perfect example. Let's say you go out for a doctor's visit. On the way home, you stop at the store and buy cat food, swing by Chipotle for a $20 dinner, and put gas in your car. It's not hard to spend money when you are traveling or leaving home all the time.

On the other hand, it's much easier to save money if you stay at home more.

Yes, you have online shopping available. If that is a problem for you, delete every payment method in your stored wallet on Amazon. Put in a pre-paid debit card for whatever amount you need to spend for online shopping. When the money is gone, it's gone.

It's not complicated. What makes it hard is that you are changing long-held habits and beliefs. Let's look at another key to help you move forward.

DETERMINING YOUR ASSETS AND INCOME

I want to point you again to the worksheet made available for you. You'll find it here:

It's a great tool to help you get a clear picture of your assets, liabilities, and income. Once you do that, you can easily grasp where you are now and how you can chart a better pathway forward.

Also, keep in mind some of the questions creditors will be asking about you. How long have you been at your job? Are you someone who is steadily employed all the time, or do you have a habit of moving around? Is your income stream year over year fairly consistent, or does it steadily rise?

Having an income that steadily rises is appealing to a creditor because it allows you to get more credit. However, it also works against you when you are trying to settle. Why? Because depending on your age, they know most people earn more income during a specific period of years. Even though you may have gotten yourself into trouble in your twenties, they know your peak earning time is coming down the road.

Creditors may look at your situation and think, *We don't want to abuse this client because we know there are useful years after we get past this little rough patch.* They may want to settle with you now for a reasonable amount, knowing they will want you again as a client when you get back on your feet. It all factors into how they deal with you.

So, income is an important factor, but so is your age and year-over-year increases. If you have moved around from job to job, they know it will be hard to garnish your wages. More than likely, they will go through the process of suing you, but then you will just quit your job and move somewhere else.

Many people don't have a true picture of their assets. They believe they have all this junk sitting around in their house when they are sitting on a small gold mine.

For example, when you go through your basement or garage, it may seem like junk to you. But there are people on eBay, Craigslist, and flea markets who will pay good money for your "junk." If you want to get through your financial mess, clean out your basement and garage and sell those items.

Back to your list of assets. If you are someone who owns a second house or has income properties, multiple cars, a boat, and off-road vehicles, creditors are going to take all that into consideration. They are going to see all that on your credit report. They will think, *This is someone who has accumulated assets, and they have probably got other stuff we are not seeing.*

In a worst-case scenario, a bankruptcy, you would be surprised at what they can take. For example, they could take your guns if you own them. You will have to disclose everything to the trustee, and they will want to liquidate as much as they can. They can also access your retirement and 401(k) accounts.

In that type of worst-case situation, they will "reassign the debt." In most cases, people still have income. However, their liabilities have exceeded their assets, so the creditor will reassign certain debts that are a priority, like your car, and you are going to keep that out of bankruptcy. At the same time, you will put everything else that you can into the bankruptcy. You could give up a lot of your assets, down to the ones you can still hang on to economically.

YOU HAVE FREEDOM OF CHOICE

As kids, we hated other people telling us what to do. Parents, teachers, siblings, authority figures . . . they all liked to "boss us around" at every opportunity. Or at least, that's how it seemed from our limited vantage point.

It can feel the same when you are going through financial problems. Creditors, trustees, counselors, banks, and anyone who has an interest in our money all seem in a hurry to tell us what to do.

But remember, you always have a choice. Each choice comes with a different set of requirements and consequences, but you still have a choice. Now that you have gotten your mindset right and analyzed your situation, which pathway will you choose?

Sometimes, the clear choice is not the one you decide to take. If the banks had total control over you, they would say, "Based on your situation, you are going to go down this road." But people have freedom of choice, so they might say, "Yeah, that looks like a good choice, but no, I don't want to do that, so I am going to choose this other path."

So, instead of credit counseling, you could choose debt settlement. It would probably not be bankruptcy, but you have to qualify for that. They can turn you away if you have the means of paying your debt. They won't allow you to file if you don't qualify. With a Chapter 7 bankruptcy, you must give everything up, including your car, but you can reassign that debt. You are basically telling them you are going to pull that out of bankruptcy and sign a new agreement with that creditor, and you are going to make a commitment.

Now, if, for some reason, you fail on the payments for whatever it is you held out of bankruptcy, you can't put that back into bankruptcy and get the protection you are looking for. You can do it after seven years since you can file for bankruptcy every seven years, but you will be at the mercy of that creditor until then. They will have all the remedies available to them to try and collect from you.

That may all feel overwhelming to you. If so, that's perfectly okay.

The main objective right now is to make sure you are getting a good, accurate look at your current situation. In the rest of the book, we will dive into several possible directions, beginning with a popular option—loan consolidation.

WHAT YOU CAN DO RIGHT NOW

- Build a budget. It might sound scary, but a budget is actually freeing! Knowing where your money is going each month is a great step to becoming financially sound.
- Stop nonessential automated payments. Review your accounts and see where you can stop any automatic payments (and how much you can save each month). You won't have to give up these expenses forever. But for now, it's time to get rid of any expenses that aren't essential, meaning job-related, food, and a place to live.

CHAPTER FIVE

LOAN CONSOLIDATION

Now that you have analyzed your situation and thought about your options, it's time to get serious about taking action. Are you ready?

If so, let's consider one of the easiest paths forward—loan consolidation. Simply put, that means taking multiple debts, applying for a loan, getting approved for that loan, then consolidating the debt into one loan with simple interest.

Almost everyone has heard of loan consolidation. It would seem like a simple solution to your financial woes because it streamlines your payments and saves you money on interest. What's not to love?

But not so fast; there is a danger that many people fall into when it comes to loan consolidation. When you go that route, it opens the lines of credit available on your credit cards. So more than likely, you are going to load up your cards again. Then you will be in a tough spot since you not only have a large primary loan but new additional credit card debt as well.

That is the reason loan consolidation companies are very selective about who gets a loan. You can have an exemplary credit score, but if you are maxed out on credit cards, you won't get a consolidation loan.

DO YOU "WALK ON WATER?"

When you're in the middle of a financial crisis, you spend a lot of time hoping for a miracle. Ironically, the loan consolidation companies practically expect you to be the one performing miracles. For that reason, that type of loan is usually called the "Jesus loan" or the "walk on water" loan.

Keep in mind that people are people. They may have tried to get a loan from one place but were turned down. That has a compounding effect because they have run your credit. Then, when you try to apply at a different place, they also do a credit check and see that you were turned down at the last place. It leaves a trail. Even people who are doing the debt snowball program have probably looked at loan consolidation. It makes sense for most people because they can make two important exchanges: converting high-interest debt to low-interest debt and exchanging compound interest for simple interest. They can also combine multiple types of debt into loan consolidation.

But by the time they get to credit counseling or debt settlement, they have probably looked at this option, which was eliminated since they could not qualify. The reason? Their debt-to-income ratio is too high. Many times, there is a reason the person needs to consolidate. That reason can range from a change in job, a decrease in wages, a spouse not working anymore, or some other situation. They may have qualified for a loan consolidation before, but they no longer do.

The underwriting is different with each loan company. There are lending underwriting guidelines, but there are all kinds of nuances within those big guidelines.

IS LOAN CONSOLIDATION RIGHT FOR YOU?

Loan consolidation is just a restructuring of debt. It is for people who have demonstrated income, who are kind of sloppy, and who haven't managed their debt very well. They probably have more credit card accounts than they need. In addition, they probably have debt in certain categories that don't have advantageous interest rates.

They have good enough credit and good enough income to leverage debt at a lower interest rate to pay off other debt currently being carried at a disadvantaged rate. It is kind of a "housecleaning."

Another group of people who are typically interested in loan consolidation are those who have lots of equity in their house. They want to take some of that out and clean up the debt. They aren't at risk of losing their job or income, or they have sufficient savings as a backup that would prevent them from defaulting on their mortgage.

Therefore, they are not at risk of losing their house as a result of adding additional debt to their mortgage in the form of a HELOC (Home Equity Line of Credit) or second mortgage.

We live in a huge country of 300+ million people. Even though lenders are very selective, it is still a big pool of people for these companies. It is also worth noting that it is like a supermarket out there. There is a lender for anyone in any situation. One lender's criteria may not necessarily be the same as another lender's criteria.

What is going to impact that criteria? Interest rate. The "walk on water" loan is ideal for people who have the lowest interest rates and highest credit score possible. They are not completely maxed out on their credit cards, and their utilization is 70% versus 99%. A person who has high utilization and average credit will have a high interest rate. Instead of 4%, it is going to be 10%, 15%, or higher.

All those come with risk. The higher your interest rate, the more you are going to struggle to make that payment. Why the high interest rate? Because they are going to get as much out of you as they can, while they can. They've done the numbers. On a high-interest-rate loan like that, the default rate is "X" versus a low interest rate, high-credit-score borrower, where the default rate is much, much lower.

Those combined factors determine where that interest rate falls. Most people assume that because they are small business owners and their taxes reflect a low tax liability, they cannot get a loan. But it all depends. A traditional bank will probably turn you down, but a nonconforming lender will be more likely to give you a loan.

Don't get locked into a limited view and bypass some options that might be right for you.

COMPARING THE POSITIVES AND NEGATIVES OF LOAN CONSOLIDATION

Let's begin with the positives. The first thing is the most obvious benefit: It will probably have a positive impact on your credit report. You are also going to have a more affordable payment.

But let's dig in a little further. You can restructure high-interest debt that compounds daily with lower interest debt that compounds with simple interest. Here is the way interest is calculated on credit card debt—you take the annual interest rate divided by 365, and that's the amount of daily interest charged. So, every day, there is a small piece of interest that gets added to your account.

The next day's interest is calculated off that new balance. It includes that little bit of interest as opposed to a simple interest calculation that takes your average balance over the month, applies an interest rate to it, adds it to your balance at the end of the month, and then, your next month's interest is calculated from that number.

Did that make your head spin? If so, you're not alone. It is a vicious cycle. That leads us to the negatives.

It is important to note that people will take equity out of their homes to pay off debt. If you use a home equity line of credit or refinance your house to pull money out to pay off debt, you are taking short-term debt and making it long-term debt. You are also taking unsecured debt and making it secured debt.

If you run the numbers on it and pay it back over thirty years versus fifteen years, you are coming out worse. On an amortized home loan, you will pay back a third of what that debt amount is. For example, if you borrow $100,000, you will pay back the $100,000 plus $33,000 over the life of that loan.

Here is where people get into trouble; now you have securitized the debt, and therefore, your home is at risk. If you can't make your mortgage payment, you could lose your house. You have also freed up your credit lines, which means you could use them again. So, you've got a higher mortgage amount and will likely load up your credit cards again.

Let's go a little further. Generally, those loans come with shorter terms, which means they have higher payments. So, a twelve-month, twenty-four-month, or thirty-six-month loan may not provide people the payment relief they need. The goal of doing it is to get payment relief.

The problem is in the way credit minimum payments are structured. People are trying to lower their interest rate, thinking, *I will pay less every month*. But here is the way credit card minimum payment is calculated;

they take 1% of your balance and then add all the penalties, interest, and fees to that. That creates your minimum payment. Only a fraction of your payment goes to the principal.

For example, if you take $10,000 in a personal loan and you break that $10,000 into twelve payments, you are paying a minimum of one-twelfth of the principal every month, plus interest on top of that. The result? You are not paying less every month—you are paying more every month.

If you are trying to free up money in your wallet every month with different debt servicing options, then adding a loan consolidation to it will not reduce the amount you pay every month.

Credit counseling won't do it either. Credit counseling is going to increase your monthly payment obligations every month. That's why people who are on the bubble, struggling to make the minimum payment every month, never qualify for credit counseling. They have already blown past that option.

With all that said, when is consolidation the right option for you?

WHEN IS LOAN CONSOLIDATION THE RIGHT OPTION?

There is a very specific window when you are a good fit for loan consolidation. Your credit must still be good. You must be able to have enough foresight to see that you need to consolidate now. You can see trouble coming, and consolidating will lower the payment and lower the amount of time being strangled by debt. That scenario is perfect for someone looking for consolidation.

But here is what happens: Most people miss the window. They wait too long until their situation is at the point where they are headed toward a cliff. And the problem is that when a bank runs your credit, they see that you are near the cliff, too.

Everyone wants a consolidation loan. They think it is going to be the answer to their problems. But as I have said, there is a very specific window when people looking for loan consolidation can fit in at the right moment and in the right situation. Most people wait too long and miss that window. They didn't think about doing the consolidation back when they should have. So, they are maxed out on their credit card debt, and there is no room.

In other words, you may be current on your payments, but you cannot pay any more than the minimums. The loan consolidation company sees the same thing—you are maxed out. If they give you a consolidation loan, that just frees up your credit line on your credit cards. Chances are very high that you will load those up again, and now they are screwed.

The short story is that loan consolidation seems like the perfect solution, but not everyone fits into that box.

A WORD ABOUT HIGH INTEREST RATES

Before we close out this chapter, it will be helpful to look at the reason behind high interest rates. What do they mean, and where do they come from? Why are they so high? Why do we have a 0% interest rate from the Fed yet 29% on a credit card?

Most people believe the answer is, "Because they can." It's natural to look at credit card companies as the enemy who only wants to screw you over. While that may be true, it doesn't explain the high interest rates.

It all comes down to you being a risk. They know a certain percentage of people are going to fail. They are high-risk. So, they know their percentages and are covering themselves.

You typically don't see a credit card at less than 15% interest anymore. They will advertise 14.9%, but that's about as low as it gets. The range goes from 14.9% to 29.9%, and it's compounded from there.

It is an especially big problem for college student debt. Credit card companies were notorious for going to colleges, putting up tents, and recruiting on campuses. They knew college students would fall for having $5,000 or $10,000 in their pocket and that they wouldn't understand compound interest.

We don't want to paint all creditors as the bad guys because we do need the banks. However, they purport themselves to be saviors who have credibility. They pretend they are looking out for your best interests when, in fact, they are only after your money.

WHO IS TO BLAME?

The honest truth is that most people have dug a hole, they sit there, and they don't know what to do. They need someone to come alongside them and tell them what is possible. Don't assume your life is over.

Maybe you feel overwhelmed and don't know what to do or where to go from here. That's okay. We are here to help guide you to the core of the problem and to help you deal with it.

Part of getting your mind right is assessing the blame. Who is to blame for the problems you are facing? Is it you, or is it your creditors? Do they share some of the blame?

They should because sometimes they can be very predatory and bury people. That may sound harsh, but the government hates predators. They don't like predatory lending. The government is very hard on payday lenders and the people who do marketplace loans, like a short-term loan, because they can be so predatory.

One interesting tidbit—have you ever noticed that the addresses of credit cards or any kind of banking are always in South Dakota? The reason is that the state allows these high interest rates. You can't charge these crazy high interest rates in other states. South Dakota law states that banks based there can charge up to 29% interest. The state needed revenue, so they passed a law allowing that interest rate. Most states have usury laws that prevent you from charging excess interest, which was waived in South Dakota.

That is just one small example of the stunts credit card companies and other lenders will pull to extract as much from you as possible. Don't believe for a moment that they are looking out for your best interests.

WHAT YOU CAN DO RIGHT NOW

- Understand and compare the positives and negatives of loan consolidation to see whether it is the right choice for you.
- Do you know your credit score? If you have a very high credit score and aren't maxed out on your credit cards, you may qualify for a "Jesus loan."

CHAPTER SIX

CREDIT COUNSELING AND DEBT MANAGEMENT

Credit counseling has been an accessible option since the 1950s. Bankers gathered around, scratching their heads, saying, "Look—we need another method for dealing with these delinquent people outside of collections." Their question became, How do we keep portfolios performing?

They were tired of fighting among themselves and trying to collect from the masses until they were forced to file bankruptcy. By unifying with a method that allowed debtors to proportionally pay them back, bankers were confident they'd be better off. Even if only 50% of consumers bought into it, they'd consider it a success. So, they created a systematic line of defense: credit counseling, collections, then selling the debt. It's all a game, and I'm here to keep you from playing it.

PORTFOLIOS OVER PEOPLE

Allow me to let you in on a little secret. Banks don't care about you. They don't care about me. They care about portfolio performance and maximization. They care about investors in portfolios, hedge funds, mutual funds, and pension funds. Their primary goal is to keep portfolios spit-shined for a significant amount of time to prevent charge-offs around the six-month period. It's something as promising as pyrite (fool's gold), but to the consumer looking to strike gold, it appears to be the answer.

The client thinks, So, you're going to call my creditors for me? Most of the time, bankers will drop their interest to zero for a while, then raise it later to a nominal amount and adjust the client's payment accordingly. The client will then make one payment to the credit counseling company to distribute the funds to the creditors.

These debt management plans repay the full amount owed over a term no greater than five years or sixty months. In exchange for participation, the creditor might reduce fees, absolve penalties, or propose a tempting interest rate that will not accrue charges quickly.

That means the client's interest rates might decrease from 19% to 11%, but it will not be a significant change overall. Meanwhile, the client will have to demonstrate they have enough income to cover their expenses and pay off the full balance, plus interest, within the allotted time. That puts distressed individuals into a slight restructure that only helps in the immediate future but likely does more damage in the long term.

What's even more complicated is that creditors play by their own rules. They sometimes come back with the condition that says, *We will not be the only party making compromises here. We will accept this account, but the consumer has to enroll these other accounts as well.*

That is what I call—a catastrophe. Do not fall for it, or else they've got you. They set the terms on these accounts, including determining their own interest rates. They have their own policies about what things they will forgive, abate, and roll back. Someone who hasn't hit rock bottom can support a bogus five-year repayment plan at the full amount plus interest. They qualify for the program easily. They demonstrate through paystubs and W-2s that they are capable. The people who are truly stuck won't get as seemingly lucky. And they are typically the group most affected—the ones who default over that five-year term and have the forgiven interest rolled back and re-calculated but with penalties and fees that were never required on the front end. It leaves people worse off than when they started. I'll say it again. Catastrophe.

For consumers with minimal debt, this might not be such a poor option. But for clients with more than $25,000 accrued, the relief just isn't there. What's worse, credit counseling has lost a lot of ground to debt settlement. The National Foundation for Credit Counseling (NFCC) is dictated by the OCC, and they regulate what can and cannot be offered to the consumer.

That has put a stumbling block between credit counselors and creditors—counselors continually appeal to the OCC to allow them to do settlements, and they are continually, rightfully, denied.

ARE YOU ELIGIBLE FOR AN EARLY CHARGE-OFF?

Banks can do what's called an *early charge-off*. It creates an exception to the rule of not beginning negotiations until ninety days have passed. If a client calls in and says, "I cannot make this payment due to life circumstances," the bank will charge the account and issue an R9 without going through the bucket process. Then, the terms will be re-determined. In some cases, banks extend the terms. That was Capital One's primary answer to debt settlement—they'd extend terms up to ten years, which inherently impacted them because they'd have to report that as a *charge-off* even earlier.

The worst damage to your credit score happens at the six-month point of nonpayment when the lender charges off your debt as a loss. From that point forward, your credit can start to heal if you do absolutely nothing to resolve it and ignore your creditors completely. It takes time, but it will jump back to a respectable number with zero effort on your part.

But here's the tricky part. If you suddenly find yourself in a less-stressed spot and have some income to devote to your old debts, you may decide to pursue repayment.

"That one collector was nice," you remember. "Maybe I should pay it off to feel better about myself so I'm not a deadbeat."

Too late. You realize that simply paying on a collection account can harm your credit, no matter how much time has lapsed.

Don't get me wrong; settling is a good thing, but it's important to consider how it will impact your credit score. Is it worth it?

Essentially, debt relief options and credit counseling fit a certain type of person—specifically someone who is unable to effectively reduce the principal amount of what they owe. Their attempt to lower their interest rates demonstrates their need for relief and is primarily about their unaffordable monthly payments. That destructive cycle can become a whirlwind for desperate consumers. Credit counselors, following the banking regulators' guidelines, elongate the confusing cycle that delays the inevitable. *Here, you have a problem, so we'll give you a solution that will help you minimally until you completely drop off the edge of a cliff.*

In reality, credit counseling companies can only offer a handful of options. They can't help everyone. Credit card debt is different than utility bills, personal loans, and medical debt. While they all have unique stages of delinquency, credit card debt is usually broken up into thirty-day brackets for up to ninety days.

If someone is in real trouble and cannot pay their bills, the best they can offer is to re-age the account if, and only if, it falls into the 1–30, 30–60, or 60–90 day age range. In most cases, the promise of a counselor holds no real weight. Let's say someone calls in with the most profound tragedy. They will sit on the other end of the phone, saying something like, "Look, my spouse died, and I just need some more time." As empathetic as they seem, the counselor's hands are essentially tied no matter how harrowing the story.

At the end of the day, they have the statute of limitations to worry about—the law is the law. No law will spare someone from the negatives, and only a few will experience the benefits of the positives.

COMPARING THE POSITIVES AND NEGATIVES OF CREDIT COUNSELING

When considering credit counseling, it is important to keep in mind that credit card companies run these programs. Credit card companies are going to produce nothing verifiable or backed by adequate statistics. If they did produce independent studies on this matter, there would be a coup. It would demonstrate the high percentage of people who do not qualify for credit counseling and an equally high amount who are unsuccessful.

If clients are already distressed and unable to make minimal payments, they will never pay off the full balance of their debt in five years when the minimum payment is based on a thirty-year repayment plan. People who truly need credit counseling, who would benefit from it, and be successful, would never apply for it because they have postured themselves for success and have more stable situations.

POSITIVES OF CREDIT COUNSELING

1. Creditors will not call clients who are on a plan of reduced interest payments.

2. Temporarily reduce your interest rates.
3. You may be able to completely pay off your debt in as little as five years.
4. Being in a program has a neutral impact on your credit score.

NEGATIVES OF CREDIT COUNSELING

1. Credit counselors downplay the negatives; they don't properly hold the client's hand through the process. Therefore, their expectation is never fully met.
2. Because that relief is so minuscule, the failure rate is extremely high—up to 60%.
3. A client can be in the program for five years or longer, which seems promising but is disastrous.
4. While clients are in the program, agencies make a notation on the client's credit report that they are in a credit counseling program, so they cannot finance anything during that period. Many people may be in a credit counseling program, and they could help themselves more by refinancing their house—but because of their choice to join the program, they can't; they're essentially screwed.
5. It's heavily dependent on the amount of debt a client has. The lower the debt amount, the better the program works, but the higher the debt amount, the more likely the client is going to be negatively impacted.

The people who take the bait are typically the *I live beyond my means, paying my minimum payments, in denial of my situation, as I strap my fake Rolex onto my wrist, get in my jellybean-looking car and go out there to impress the masses* type. Good for them. They may go to credit counseling and get one or two accounts accepted, but they will certainly be struggling elsewhere because, guaranteed, they are taking the accumulation of five cards and putting them on two out-of-control cards. That does not address the core problem.

Pretty soon, they'll have late payments and dings on their credit score. So, when they return to loan consolidation, they are convinced they just need more money on the loan, then quickly find out they are only going to get a twelve-month term, with a 22–31% interest rate that doesn't solve their problem.

Their debt and poor decisions beget more debt, hopelessness, and poorer decisions. Eventually, that *type* of person will throw their hands up and say, "Screw it! I'm done playing the game. I'm just going to go file Chapter 7 bankruptcy and get rid of my debt."

Then, they'll go into the bankruptcy program and be forced to recognize that they cannot pass the means test in their state. Because, most likely, they make too much money. They have too many assets. They realize that to get all of their debt discharged in bankruptcy, they are going to have to sell their car, which is worth $25,000, because they are only going to be able to keep one car that is worth $4,000 or less and use the proceeds to pay off their debt.

They'll sell their house and go live in an apartment for one to three years until they can afford to purchase a home again, not realizing that the bankruptcy is going to stay on their credit report for ten years, which ultimately means they will be stuck in that apartment for a decade. It's because somewhere, they've heard of people who file bankruptcy and get to do things like keeping their house. But they do not understand it is a formula based at the state level, and every state has a different means test, income test, and asset test, so what they are really looking at is deferred hope.

IF IT SOUNDS TOO GOOD TO BE TRUE . . .

In finance, a good rule of thumb is to question anything that sounds like an immediate solution—if it sounds too good to be true, it is. I write this to help readers avoid empty promises and not chase dead ends. Mental health studies demonstrate the hopelessness attributed to mounting debt—statistics back high numbers of suicide due to accumulation of material objects and mishandled money. I don't want that to be you, and if you're in a powerless place at the moment, I don't want you to be duped by those who do not have your best interest at heart. The mindset behind all financial planning must be a long game. If the only temporary benefit is fewer phone calls from obnoxious debt collectors, I say throw your phone out the window and come up with a better plan because that is no significant benefit at all. It's time to put the gold Rolex away and dream bigger than a jellybean car.

The first step is admitting there is an issue; the second step is accessing the appropriate tools to fix it. This book can supply the necessary tools, but I come by the solution honestly. No, this will not be quick and easy, but when you reach financial relief on the other side, you will be grateful you took the more challenging approach.

WHAT YOU CAN DO RIGHT NOW

- Accept the hard truth that banks are businesses, and they don't care about you. They do care about performance, maximization, and collecting their money.
- Review the negatives and positives of credit counseling to see if it is the best option for you.
- Remember, if a financial solution sounds too good to be true, it is likely not going to be helpful to your progress. Slow and steady wins the race.

CHAPTER SEVEN

DEBT SETTLEMENT

Believe it or not, debt settlement goes back to biblical times. The Debt Jubilee in the Bible consists of the consumer's debt being forgiven every seven years. I have to imagine that human behavior doesn't change that much. I'm sure, back then, people would run up their debt knowing if they could hold out for seven years and someone didn't chop their hand off, they'd be okay. Then there were probably others who were horrified of debt, and they'd work their butts off to pay it back.

Creditors have always been the same—total sharks. At best, there are those people out there who look for any crack in the armor they can find and exploit it, and banks know that. In the present day, there are those who advocate for the poor consumer, like the Consumer Financial Protection Bureau, but they typically do not take into account the shysters who try to take advantage of the banks.

When consumers are desperate, they begin looking for the radical options mentioned throughout these sections. Loan consolidation is probably the number one thing they look for first. What happens is kind of a catch-22. After doing minimal research, the consumer often calls a company who, more often than not, will pitch debt settlement because their loan criteria are so strict that only a small number of people qualify for these loans.

In turn, people get enrolled in debt settlement programs. Nevertheless, by the end of the term, they fall back into old habits. They'll make their last payment, and then their world will be flooded with credit card offers again. Those who have learned their lesson say, "No, I'm never getting into credit card debt again," while also realizing they are going to have to dance with their demons to some degree because they will need to maintain their credit score and keep at least one card for minimal use. But most people are like the guy willing to get his hand cut off between the seven-year bookends of debt relief. He's the guy willing to buy the cup of coffee even if his card has been declined. These people will go through the cycle of debt more than once in their lifetime. They learn by failing over and over again—and after chaotic stints of being in a broke panic, they become addicted to the cycle.

That is why it's imperative to understand that money is always going to be about mindset. Your mind is the one thing that will keep you coming back. Understanding the power dynamics of the system and its intricacies can prevent a heap of hurt if you're willing to advocate for yourself. If you're going to lend energy to collectors you owe—do it with agency, dignity, and a plan.

All of us have the right to dispute any debt we may have because there are a lot of unscrupulous people out there who will try to collect on a debt that is either legally uncollectible or doesn't even belong to us.

The more knowledge you have about your rights and how the industry operates, the better off you'll be.

THE DEBT SETTLEMENT PROCESS

Let's start with the basic premise of a debt settlement company in which the consumer enrolls their debts and is started on an affordable payment plan. That money is set aside in a third-party trust account to protect the consumer. The money will continue to accrue until the eventual settlement with creditors. At the time of enrollment, the settlement company will analyze your financial situation, consider your hardship, ability to pay, and potentially your assets and liabilities. Depending on your situation, you could be placed in a program for anywhere from twenty-four to forty-eight months.

For the duration of the program, as monies are set aside, the settlement companies can approach the creditors on your behalf and request settlement terms. Armed with huge amounts of trust money that have accumulated, plus all the financial data from thousands of their consumers, these companies can get settlement offers for a fraction of what is owed. As settlement offers come in, the consumer is notified and has the ability to approve or decline the settlement offer. Once an offer is accepted, depending upon whether it is a term settlement or lump sum, the payment will be distributed by the payment processor.

Keep in mind, the typical debt settlement client, before signing up, is current on their payments but can see the edge of the cliff coming up fast. But they still have the means to make larger monthly payments and can set aside a reasonable amount of money.

In theory, you can settle your debts on your own; you don't need a settlement company to do it for you. Most people, however, don't have the knowledge or time to wait out their creditors or want to deal with them.

Again, creditors have tactics to make you feel less than human if you aren't paying your debt off in full, even if you have a reason. The banks would prefer that you have proof of a legitimate hardship to settle with you, but if you can't pay and you are at the end of your rope, they will often choose to settle. In reality, anyone at any time can choose to settle their debt and deal with the consequences and fall out.

KNOWING THE INS AND OUTS OF DEBT CAN SAVE YOU TIME, MONEY, AND SANITY

While I would always recommend hiring an expert to help you navigate debt repayment and negotiation, it's important that you know the intricacies of debt and how creditors operate so you can fly solo if you need to. One of the key elements to being able to do that is getting your mind right. Say it with me, "It's not my fault." It's really not—there is blame to share all around. You want to be on equal footing when you talk to these people because when talking to someone we owe, the tendency is to feel shame or guilt and shrink. It makes the consumer smaller than the creditor—*I want to pay you back!* But, if your mindset is, *Well, you kind of gouged me in the process here; you kept raising my interest rate every time, and I couldn't get ahead—you, too, are to blame,* the footing is more leveled out, and you can both discuss what is fair to you. It's about taking back control.

Spread the blame around where it belongs. It's a group effort to compound debt. Every month, when you wanted to pay your debt, you paid the $100 minimum—but they didn't tell you that $100 wouldn't go very far because of stipulations hidden in the fine print and insane interest rates.

The goal is to remember that they don't have a hold on you. There is nothing to be afraid of, especially these days when there are many more regulations preventing harassment. Many things have changed over the last decade. There are certain stories that have frustrated me and have stayed with me throughout my career. For example, I once worked with an elderly couple who were so overwhelmed with fear of their collectors that they would beg me to speak for them. They'd say things like, "I'm just too scared to talk to them," or "The collectors have already said if I don't pay, they will take our home."

In situations where people cannot shake the anxiety, I recommend bringing in the professionals; they can reign everything in. Whatever you do, don't sit on it out of fear—it's better to have someone make the calls for you early in the process than end up having to file for bankruptcy when it might have been avoidable.

DON'T FALL FOR FEAR

Fear is an ineffective motivator. It makes people do unbalanced things. Many people will let go of their cars and homes but will keep paying their credit cards because they want to keep using them. People think they can't do anything without having their credit cards. We saw examples of this with the last national banking and housing crisis when people had access to easy money. After 2020, we'll see it again. There are forbearances, abatements, and evictions combined with stimulus money and long-term unemployment. We are on the brink of what I believe will be an even bigger disaster.

Sure, without a credit card you can't book flights or hotel rooms—we live in a society where consumers are almost forced to have a credit card, which messes with their equilibrium because it puts them in a place below lenders. It makes people dupable. It's predatory and a complete headache.

That is why the stimulus checks issued by the federal government after the COVID-19 pandemic will be used in unexpected ways. When consumers get money like that, they will use it to pay their credit card debt. So, in economic crises, credit card debt goes down, which is odd because the effect of paying that credit card down raises everyone's credit score, but in reality, they are not financially strong.

Paying down your credit card or unsecured debt sounds good. However, you have people who are living off borrowed money—free money, I should say. The buzz in the industry is that it is a false-positive. We have people who are using money from the government to pay their credit card debt down, and it's making their credit score go up, but their credit score shouldn't go up because we know, when the stimulus stops, they are in the same position.

Now, they are talking about dragging this out and continuing to pay unemployment and other stimulus monies, possibly into 2022. At some point, the music is going to stop, and it is going to be bad. I think we are in the eye of the storm. It is calm right now. But I anticipate that we will see the cracks start to show in a year or so. We had the lowest number of bankruptcies we have had in a long time. Normally, it's around 900,000 to 1.1 million filings a year. In 2020, it was at half of that—500,000. But I know for every high, there will be an equal and opposite low.

WHEN IS THE RIGHT TIME TO SETTLE?

All that begs the question, when is it the best time for debt settlement? I think it gets situational. Do you have one debt? Is it a utility bill? A personal loan? Is it current?

If you have multiple debts, it changes everything because then you have to prioritize.

For example, if you have six different creditors and you don't know which one is going to settle first, the default way to think about it is, *I will just attack the smallest debt first because I will be able to save up for that one quicker*, but it usually doesn't work that way.

Because there are many different types of debt, every scenario is different. For example, credit card debt is different from medical debt; personal loan debt is different from utility debt and store cards. Credit cards are governed by the FDIC's *Credit Card Activities Manual*. That governs what credit card companies can do and when they can do it.

If there's only a single account, I would suggest breaking it down into categories: *current, delinquent,* or *in collections*. I make the distinction between *delinquent* and *in collections* because you could have missed a couple of payments that might not have been sent to collections yet.

Forget credit cards for a minute. Let's use your phone service, for example. They don't collect in-house. When you go delinquent, after a period of time, they send you a notice saying, "Hey, you are behind," and normally, people pay it because they want to maintain their service.

But let's say you move away and don't care anymore, so you let it go, and it's turned into a collection account. You've moved across the country and use a totally different service, and you've forgotten about it, but then you get this collection letter saying you owe us this money. In turn, how you handle it when it's delinquent is different from how you handle it if it's a collection account. If it's delinquent, there is not going to be a discount. It cannot be settled for a percentage of the principal balance. Collection accounts, in this scenario, are totally different.

With phone companies, there are hundreds of thousands of people who fall into this category—whose accounts have been sent to collections. So, they package up people statewide or regionwide and send them to a collection agency or a collection law firm to collect on those accounts.

When phone companies do that, they generally give the collection agency or collection law firm guidelines on how they want the people to be treated and what their allowable settlement authorities are. They do that for future business because they don't want to hammer the client in case they can have them as a client again in the future. They don't want them to have a completely bad experience.

Depending on the company's financial situation, they may be more lenient or harsh—it's about how much they want the money. Additionally, from a strictly business standpoint, they have to make an effort to try and collect on those outstanding receivables. If you're in another state, are they really going to pressure you that hard to settle? Maybe they'll take twenty cents on the dollar and call it a day. Again, the consumer has all the power.

MULTIPLE DEBTS BETWEEN CREDIT CARDS

Now, let's get into the more difficult one, the typical scenario people are in. They have heavy credit card debt, and they've started to get upside down because either they are overextended on the credit card or they have some medical event.

I estimate that 80% of the time, debt is medically related. So, there will be medical debt on top of the credit card debt, and those two things will settle differently. Medical debt is much harder to collect. There are a lot more nuances because, most of the time, insurance is involved, and the insurance company is picking up some of the cost. It typically gets muddled—what is your part as the consumer, and what is their part as an insurance company.

So, let's say a person has six credit cards; it might even be higher on average than the industry sees. Nationwide, it is probably an average of two-and-a-half cards per household.

The factors that determine how we are going to approach this are:

1. The balance on each card.
2. The type of creditor that owns that card.
3. The ability of the consumer to set aside the proper amount of funds in a reasonable amount of time.

Say you have one credit card that has an $800 balance, and you may have another credit card that has a $15,000 balance. Those two extremes create a balance of $15,800. The goal then is to come up with a budget and set aside the money for those accounts.

Let's say you set aside $500 a month, and you are three months into this process—that's $1,500 ready to go. You might have an $800 card sitting there and the hope of settling it for $400, but the credit card company says they are not going to deal with you right now. You might want to go after the bigger credit card, but they won't allow you to pay on it until you have more funds to attack it. They may decide that they are just not settling right now, or they say they will only take payment in full, $800, or 90% of it.

Those are the types of scenarios you get when dealing with multiple creditors. Sometimes they don't make any logical sense.

CALLING YOUR CREDITORS

We will get into the mechanics for your day one of this process on what each case study could look like. But, as you can imagine, banks are huge. A consumer could call in many times and talk to a hundred different people. Sometimes, you have to dig in and find that empathy—there is always some element of personality involved.

If the consumer can find a little crack in the facade and get someone to listen, it'll help facilitate the conversation. Remember, as a consumer, you can control the conversation. If you don't hear what you like the first time, just hang up and call again. That is what happens in a debt settlement company. They are used to it!

If you're going to go rogue, understand that you're going to be chased. It becomes nauseating to look at your phone and have your voicemail flooded. That taunting always yields a response—even when we don't want it to. That's why it's important to know your strategy. Remember, collection agencies aren't set up to be a paper mill—they are simply set up to collect as much debt as they can. That's why, if you put everything in writing instead of online, things are harder to trace. Sometimes, when you ask collectors to validate your debt, they will send you a piece of paper saying, *yep, you owe this money!* If you have something to bite back with, like, "That's not going to cut it. Show me some proof! I want to see the contract I signed"—you're going to have much more leverage.

If, by chance, they *can* provide that because it's in your portfolio of debt, it comes down to you saying, "Alright, let's work out a settlement." You need to have a story together about your hardship and why they should settle for whatever you are asking to pay.

As a result, they might get a settlement of zero or pennies on the dollar. Usually, if it's a terminal illness, it's a family member calling. Situations of potential suicide and extreme mental distress are almost always automatic since that has a behavioral health component to it. The consumer will be required to have a wellness check-up, but the collection activity will automatically stop. There is a list of *trigger words* banks keep in the collections and recovery department. They help creditors determine critical scenarios and respond more sensitively if there are mental or physical health issues. These are considered potential terminal breaks.

If a terminal break is allowed due to hardship, dealing with an agency can become even more convoluted. When a bank sends a portfolio to the collection agency, all types of parameters are included.

There are multiple stages of collection. The first time the original creditor sends your account to a collection agency, it is called *first placement*. When they recall it and send it out a second time, it is called *second placement*. When they recall it and send it out a third time, it's called *tertiary*.

Normally, after the third placement, they will pull it back, let it sit, and decide what they want to do. They may sell it as tertiary paper to someone, and the price dictates the worth of the debt.

So, back to our poor consumer who is just trying to settle these accounts. They might be in dire straits, saying things like, "I know your settlement authority is telling you this, but I'm telling you this is all I can do, and I am borrowing the money on top of that from friends and family to pay you."

They will take that information, communicate it back to the bank, get an exception on your account, and make you that offer. That payment can be structured as a lump sum or for as many months as they are willing to let you go. Normally, it depends on the debt and other factors. It used to be six months max, and now, I've seen them stretch it out to twenty-four months. Keep in mind: Longer-term payment plans always land consumers in more hardship than it's worth.

DEBT SETTLEMENT COMPANIES CAN DO BETTER

Debt settlement programs don't always have the consumer's best interest at heart. What would it look like if they actually worked for our benefit, though?

Imagine using the first four to six months prior to the accounts falling into charge-off to take a forensic look at how we spend money. What if, for the first three months of the program, we still took that full minimum payment balance and made our first three deposits in our trust account at the full level of what we would have been making at our minimum? Then, for the next three months, we make 75% of our minimum payment so that by the seventh month of the program, we're down to 50% of our minimum payment. That simple switch from normal program payments of between 50% and 60% of our combined minimum payment accelerates the options that are available when our accounts become distressed—at the point when we are able to extract the most leverage in settling an account.

Imagine refining expenses and gamifying the journey on the front end of the program, giving participants five opportunities in the first five months of the program to find additional money in their budgets.

"More money?" you ask, incredulous. "We don't have money! That's why we're in this mess!"

Well, what about a garage sale? Clean out your closets and attics and try to get $300 from that garage sale, depositing that directly into your trust account. Then, in addition to the full minimum payment, you're putting $300 more than the minimum.

Doesn't this sound like a much more effective option than simply enrolling consumers and advising them to make level payments of 50% of the minimums across the board?

Usually, the amount of relief someone in credit debt needs is a few hundred dollars. It's the difference between struggling and comfortably surviving from one month to the next. These debt settlement companies create an unrealistic payment, where the amount of time it takes someone to get out of the debt is neither a benefit to the consumer nor the creditors.

"You promised you could get me out of debt! You haven't done a thing!"

And the debt settlement company replies, "Well, you haven't saved enough money."

Make no mistake. There will be pain and damage to your credit if you choose the debt settlement route; it's the debt settlement process to help you get through it as quickly as possible while minimizing the damage.

What I have learned is that most consumers enter debt settlement programs with an average credit score of 700 to 720. Regardless of their debt, they are making payments every month. They've got the plate spinning and the balls in the air, and they're rocking and rolling. They've got the head-turning car and the iconic watch, and they're looking the part.

The debt settlement company assures them that they will settle their debt at about half of what is owed. That sounds amazing, but it's only part of the story. What they fail to disclose is that approximately 25% of what the consumer owes will get added on top of that in fees. They're still getting a 25% break on their debt, and the bottom line is that most or all their debt is going to be paid off at the end of the program.

More good news. You can usually keep your credit card while enrolled in a debt settlement program. The alternative could destroy your career if you need to buy airplane tickets, rent cars, and book hotel rooms for work. That is not always a guarantee, though. While credit card companies can no longer apply a blanket penalty rate from card to card, they can reduce or close credit lines at any time for any reason. They can't change your interest rate because they view you as a credit risk, but they can decrease your $10,000 limit to $2,000.

Budgeting and debt reduction are not sexy terms, but ending the stress-filled existence of avoiding phone calls and holding your breath every time you use your credit card sounds pretty darn desirable.

COMPARING THE POSITIVES AND NEGATIVES OF DEBT SETTLEMENT

Think debt settlement is right for you? Here are the pros and cons so you can decide if this avenue is your best option.

POSITIVES OF DEBT SETTLEMENT:

1. It is a non-bankruptcy solution for certain people.
2. The consumer will pay back less than their original amount in a shorter amount of time—possibly being out of debt in four years or less, as opposed to fifteen-plus years.
3. Being able to set aside a manageable monthly payment to repay your creditors.

NEGATIVES OF DEBT SETTLEMENT:

1. Creditors and collectors may continue to call you.
2. Short-term negative impact on your credit.
3. Possibility of lawsuits.

BANKRUPTCY AND LAWSUITS

After years of flurried activity—phone calls, letters, and chaos—consumers may see the activity subside because they have become *uncollectible*. Then, without fail, they'll be bombarded once again, like a wild game of whack-a-mole. At that point, they can ignore the pursuits because their account hit the statute, or it's been so long their amount has fallen off their credit report.

Understand, if you get sued, the game isn't over. It means they want to talk to you and can't get a hold of you so that is the only way they have to communicate with you. In that situation, you have options. You can either settle out with favorable terms or hire an attorney. There are a lot of attorneys who take cases like these pro bono. There are nonprofit groups as well who can help those who have gotten sued.

Most people don't go to court because they are too afraid. But if a consumer shows up in court, judges are usually very lenient and pro-consumer. They will normally say to the creditor, "You two go out in the hallway and figure this out and come back and tell me what your resolution is. If you can't, I am going to come up with one that you probably won't like." They see it so much that they have a heart for people who are in desperate situations. And after the judge wipes the slate clean, creditors can't come back to you.

If a person chooses not to show up, the creditor can get a default judgment in place where the nightmare can start to happen. Then, they start looking for assets—the first place they will check is the consumer's bank account. Their primary goal is wage garnishment, and in extremely rare cases, property acquisition, which is why I recommend to clients in difficult situations to have their properties homesteaded. We don't want them taking the kitchen sink!

BORROWING

I'm often asked if borrowing money from friends and family is a good idea versus continuing in debt. My response is always the same. It comes down to personal choice. Some financial advisors insist that money is energy or spiritual. I believe it is a combination of education, discipline, a game face, and playing it smart.

Every person's dynamic with peers and blood relatives is different, so I tend to point the client back to themselves with the gentle reminder, *There are more ways to be in debt than just one! Choose wisely.*

WHAT YOU CAN DO RIGHT NOW

- I can't say it enough—your mindset will make or break you when it comes to money. Think about whether you have the interest, energy, and desire to deal with creditors yourself or if you'd rather find a partner who will advocate on your behalf.
- If you decide to borrow money from family or friends to pay down a debt, make sure you have an agreement and all applicable details in writing.
- Review the negatives and positives of the debt settlement process to see if it is the best option for you.

CHAPTER EIGHT

WHAT IS BANKRUPTCY?

Once you have become delinquent on your credit card bills, bankruptcy is a way to eliminate or reorganize your debt so you can have a clean slate. It will stop the harassing creditor calls and halt any legal action against you.

There are roughly seventy-seven million people in this country who have at least one account in collections at any given time. On average, of those seventy-seven million people, a million will turn into a Chapter 7 bankruptcy, and another million will turn into a Chapter 13 bankruptcy.

Some types of debt relief come with consequences that are more damaging and longer lasting than others.[2] But before declaring bankruptcy, it is most important to obtain information on all the options available to you to fully understand the impact those choices will have on your overall future financial picture.

The problem is that most of the information out there is not "actionable," meaning it doesn't prepare you for the specific things you need to do to get out of your situation. If you have read this book all the way to the bankruptcy chapter, you are definitely in a situation that needs a remedy.

HOW DID BANKRUPTCY ORIGINATE?

Imagine falling behind on your monthly minimum credit card payments because your hours were cut at your full-time job, and at some

---
2 "How to Get Out of Debt," Experian, https://www.experian.com/blogs/ask-experian/credit-education/how-to-get-out-of-debt/.

point, you can't even pay on your credit cards at all. Now, picture being thrown into jail because of it! From the late 1600s to the early 1800s, people who couldn't pay their debts were incarcerated, which doesn't seem like the best solution since it prevents the debtor from being able to work and make money to pay the debt. And not only were you forced to pay your debt but your prison fees also. These "debtors' prisons" were deemed archaic and were federally abolished in the United States in 1833, leaving each state to follow suit individually.

Bankruptcy was created for people in such a financial crisis who couldn't pay their creditors under the original terms to quickly end the cycle. The first three Bankruptcy Acts were in response to economic depressions and were unpopular and short-lived. All three were repealed.

The Bankruptcy Act of 1800 was very much pro-creditor and only allowed involuntary bankruptcies where a creditor could force a debtor into bankruptcy. Individuals could not file for relief voluntarily. It was repealed due to corruption and excessive fees.

The Bankruptcy Law of 1841 was the next bankruptcy law to be passed and leaned more toward the side of the debtor by allowing both merchants and non-merchants to voluntarily file to protect themselves. It was repealed mostly due to creditor dissatisfaction.

The Bankruptcy Act of 1867 permitted petitions from individuals, not just merchants, but was eventually repealed due to much of the same disapproval as earlier bankruptcy laws. All of these repeals by the federal government left solvency to the states during the in-between periods.

The Bankruptcy Act of 1898 was a turning point in American bankruptcy law and became a permanent fixture. Since then, there have been many amendments, but there have been no appeals or periods where there was no federal bankruptcy law in place. This act was definitely more in support of the debtor's interests instead of creditors. Reforms of this law have done things like increasing the power of bankruptcy judges and introducing education courses for debtors.

By the early 2000s, the average number of people filing for bankruptcy was just over 1.5 million. In 2005, that number soared to *more than two million filings*. The catalyst for the jump was the Bankruptcy Abuse Prevention and Consumer Protection Act of 2005 (BAPCPA), which was slated to introduce new requirements for bankruptcy and make it harder to file.

Passing BAPCPA made it tougher to declare personal bankruptcy. People who wanted to file also had to enroll in and attend a mandatory credit counseling class before filing and a financial management class after filing. Before that overhaul, petitioners could choose the type of bankruptcy that fit them best, and most chose to file Chapter 7 (liquidation) instead of Chapter 13 (repayment).

The 2005 law required that filers pass a means test so high-income earners would have to repay at least a portion of their debt in Chapter 13. As of the end of 2019, average Chapter 7 bankruptcy filings were one million a year, and Chapter 13s were 1.3–1.5 million a year. As mentioned previously, in America, at any given time, there are seventy-seven million people who have at least one account in collections and are on the verge of bankruptcy.

WHAT IS A CHAPTER 13 BANKRUPTCY?

A Chapter 13 "reorganization bankruptcy" or "the wage earner's plan" is for those who don't qualify for a Chapter 7 and make enough money to make payments to their creditors. It is for those who have a steady income but are delinquent on debts that secure assets, and the petitioner wants to keep those assets. It is like a debt settlement program, although it is administered by a trustee of the court. The trustee considers all assets and liabilities and does some math to determine what the petitioner needs to survive. Then, they apply what they make above and beyond that to secured creditors (first priority) and unsecured creditors (whatever is left).

A payment plan is set up and the petitioner pays the court, who then disperses it to the creditors as the plan calls for. During that time, the trustee and the creditors have a grip on the consumer for however long it takes to fulfill the plan. It could be three years, five years, or longer.

One positive is that the creditor collections and court proceedings stop immediately. Also, certain types of property are protected. Petitioners may keep property such as a home or vehicle. A notation of the bankruptcy will stay on the credit report for seven years, and the petitioner will not be able to apply for new credit until all debts have been fully discharged.

Even after the debts are discharged, it will be hard to obtain new credit until the Chapter 13 drops off the credit report. Debts that are not discharged in a Chapter 13 include things like alimony or child support, mortgage (assuming you keep the house), taxes owed, educational loans, and other monies owed due to lawsuits, criminal restitution, and fraud.

WHAT IS A CHAPTER 7 BANKRUPTCY?

A Chapter 7 "liquidation bankruptcy" is pretty straightforward. Once the trustee approves it and it is signed off by the courts, the petitioner is done. They are not required to pay qualifying debts owed to their creditors. A trustee is assigned to the person filing, and they will evaluate finances and assets for debt repayment and then discharge any remaining qualified debts. There is an allowance to keep some property to prevent destitution.

To qualify, standardized income requirements must be met to make sure that earnings are less than the median income in that specific state based on the size of the household, or the petitioner must pass a means test that assesses income, debt, and monthly expenses to prevent debts from being discharged if the petitioner could repay at least a portion of what they owe their creditors. Be aware that owning a home with more than $25,150 in equity or a vehicle worth more than $4,000 could require selling the property to pay creditors unless it can be claimed as an exemption. Debts incurred before the bankruptcy was filed can be included in the Chapter 7.

Child support and alimony, student loans, any monies owed due to "willful and malicious" injury to another person or property, monies owed due to DWI or DUI, tax debts, and debts that were not included in the filing are among the types of debts that cannot be discharged.

It typically takes four to six months to go through this type of bankruptcy, and it remains on the credit report for ten years. During that time, it is difficult to open new credit cards or get a personal loan, and getting a new mortgage or car loan will likely come with a very high interest rate.

WHAT YOU SHOULD KNOW (BUT PROBABLY DON'T) BEFORE YOU FILE BANKRUPTCY

When you are to the point that you are considering bankruptcy, you are at the point where you either a) don't want to deal with the stress anymore, or b) you physically and mentally cannot deal with the stress anymore.

That's what happens with people who are in debt. They get overwhelmed. They see the cliff coming at them at one hundred miles an hour. They assess all their options and then decide, "I'm not making enough money, the penalty rates are kicking in, the late charges are hitting me at $35 to $55 a month, I'm now paying 29.99% interest on a $10,000 credit card balance, and of my $500 a month payment, $83 is going to reduce my principal. So, I am paying $5,000 in interest a year, which means my credit card balance is going to increase by 50% in twelve months."

Most people don't even go to that level of granularity, but soon, they are slapped in the face with the reality that they are just not doing enough and don't have enough resources. So, what do they do? They solve the problem by going to the web to get a partial loan or to open another credit card, getting another credit line to try to do a balance transfer from a 29% interest rate to a 0% six-month introductory rate. They find out pretty quickly that they didn't act fast enough.

You might already be using 90% of your available credit. You've already missed a couple of payments, which has dinged your credit score fifty to seventy-five points. No one is going to give you a 0% interest rate credit card, and no one is going to give you the 5.99% partial-loan interest rate on the front page of their website.

You might get a personal loan, and you might get a simple interest calculation versus a daily periodic compounding interest charge, but you are still going to end up paying 18–22% or more, which isn't solving your problem. It is just putting a tourniquet on it.

That is where people usually start. Then, when they find out they can't do that, and they look at how much they owe and how much they make, the next thing they do is go right to the worst-case scenario. They become destitute and depressed. They decide, "I'm going to just file for bankruptcy and tell all these people to go stuff it."

So, they start looking at bankruptcy and then later find out they can't get rid of their tax debt in bankruptcy, or they can't get rid of their student loans in bankruptcy. They realize they'll trash their credit report and put someone else in charge of their checking account who is going to watch every dollar they spend. They will have to liquidate their house and their vehicles and buy a $4,000 beater that they are going to have to drive around for ten years, hoping it doesn't die. "No, I'm not doing that," they quickly decide.

Then limbo sets in. They throw their hands in the air and believe there is nothing they can do. And the mail piles up. And piles up. If you only knew on the very front end, when you first knew you were wading into troubled waters, all of the nuances about each debt relief option, you could have made a logical, informed decision that would fit your lifestyle and situation.

What you should know about bankruptcy is that it provides the big sigh of relief you have needed so badly, but it certainly doesn't come without consequences that you will live with for years to come and possibly the rest of your life. Everywhere you turn, someone will try to *sell* you a solution—their solution.

I want you to do the research and arrive at the best program for you.

I don't know how many times I have talked to someone *after* they have filed bankruptcy, and they said to me, "If I had only known (insert any number of things), I wouldn't have filed bankruptcy!" Remember, I said the same thing.

Each person reading this will have short-term financial goals and long-term financial considerations, which should both factor in to determine which path is best for them. Below is a list of some things no one mentions to you at the outset of filing bankruptcy but may be important to your specific scenario.

NEGATIVES OF BANKRUPTCY

Being treated like a child. Most bankruptcies are Chapter 13, the wage earner's plan. The trustee will take all your income, all your liabilities, all your assets, then prioritize secured debt versus unsecured debt, and your creditors are going to get in line to be paid—secured first, on down the list. Some unsecured creditors may get zero or very little. You are going to be in your plan, monitored by the trustee, for five to seven years.

During that time, you have someone telling you what you can and can't do. You have to get everything approved through the trustee for purchases. You will get a certain allowance for ancillary stuff, but you will live on a budget. You can't purchase a car, and if you need one, you have to get it approved through the trustee and justify why you need it.

A high percentage of people fail their first time around in a Chapter 13. So, your trustee and attorney have worked out a plan that says you can do x, y, and z. Then, something out of your control changes your situation. You have another incident happen, medical or otherwise, and it throws the plan you were on out the window, so you will reattempt to either move to a Chapter 7 liquidation, or they will reorganize your debts again to come up with another plan. That means you could be in this thing for a long time.

Bankruptcy is a matter of public record for the rest of your life (people mistakenly think it is just ten years). It most definitely has an impact. It used to be when you filled out an application for credit or a mortgage, they would ask, "Have you filed bankruptcy in the last seven years?" because that is how long it would stay on your credit report. (And they say *seven*, but it stays on there for ten).

Now, most creditors have modified that sentence and ask, "Have you ever filed for bankruptcy?" So, even though it may not be on your credit report anymore, you have to truthfully answer, "Yes, I did," and then you have to explain why. Is it a big deal? It depends. If you are applying for credit, it could impact the interest rate you get.

If you are applying for a job, there are a lot of positions you would be disqualified from because you have a bankruptcy on your record. So, if you don't have to do it, and there is a non-bankruptcy solution available to you, you definitely don't want to file bankruptcy. That should be what I call the "nuclear option."

Your retirement or 401k money is not always safe in bankruptcy. Although most retirement accounts are protected in bankruptcy, there are certain cases where they are not. For instance, if you were to withdraw money from your retirement account to purchase an asset or simply deposit it into your bank account before you file for bankruptcy, that money will not be protected from becoming part of the bankruptcy estate, which the court has the power to distribute to your creditors.

You now must get a credit counseling certificate to file for bankruptcy. Prior to 2005, you could just go file a straight Chapter 7 and wash your hands of everything. Then, they started creating a means test, and that is where credit counseling comes in. You have to get a certificate first to be able to file for bankruptcy. That means you have to go to a credit counseling company and go through their course, get a certificate that says you are qualified to file bankruptcy, and then file for bankruptcy. They will determine which route is best for you during that process—Chapter 13 or Chapter 7.

You may have to give up many or all your assets. You will have to disclose everything to the trustee, and the trustee will want to liquidate. The worst-case scenario in bankruptcy is they will "reassign the debt." Assuming you still have income but your liabilities have exceeded your assets, they will reassign certain debts that are a priority, like your car. You can keep that out of bankruptcy and put everything else that you possibly can in the bankruptcy. You will likely have to give up a lot of your assets down to the ones you can still hang on to economically.

To file a Chapter 7, you have to pass a means test. Before the means test, you have to determine whether your income is less than or equal to the median state income for your size household. If it is less, you can file a Chapter 7. If it is more, you have to pass a means test to assess whether you can make the payments required for a Chapter 13 with your disposable income. There is an amount set, and if your disposable income is less than that amount, you are permitted to file a Chapter 7.

More often than not, people fail in a Chapter 13 because they can't abide by the terms. Any disruption to income can throw a wrench in the repayment schedule. It is tough to go the full term of bankruptcy without credit for things like new tires on your car, a major pet illness, insurance deductibles, or even a vacation. For many people, five years of a strict repayment plan is nearly impossible, but they want relief so badly when they are filing that they don't consider that. Those are just a few of the reasons why roughly two out of three Chapter 13 cases fail.

Bankruptcy gives you a financial blemish (for insurance rates, security clearance, background checks for hiring in which you can be eliminated, etc.). Even though the Fair Credit Reporting Act says that bankruptcy filings cannot be reported in things like pre-employment screenings after ten years, and you should be protected from discrimination, simply put, they are a matter of public record and can be easily found. Even though it would be illegal for a potential employer not to hire you due to a bankruptcy filing in your past, in certain cases, it is okay to consider bad credit when a job involves money or merchandise. At the very least, you will have to defend your decision to file.

A Chapter 13 is typically a five-year ordeal. The length of a repayment plan is based on the amount and types of debt, income, and assets. People with above-average incomes typically qualify for a five-year plan. If you have no extra disposable income to make higher payments, a shorter period is likely not possible. The good thing is that Chapter 13 plans can't last longer than five years by law.

POSITIVES OF BANKRUPTCY

The "automatic stay" is a legal process that stops all collection activity. Once you have a file number for bankruptcy, your attorney will send that to your creditors, which stops all collection activity. It stops all calls. It stops everything until the trustee, working with your attorney and the courts, determines if you are going to straight liquidation or if you are going to have some sort of payment program. Usually, people just get so harassed and overwhelmed that they jump to bankruptcy to stop the ensuing madness.

Chapter 7 can liquidate all your debt. In 2005, they passed a bankruptcy reform act, which made it much more difficult to file for a straight liquidation, Chapter 7. Now, you have to go through the process of qualifying for Chapter 7. The beneficiaries of that were the credit counseling companies.

WHEN DO I KNOW IT IS TIME TO FILE BANKRUPTCY?

You never *have to* file bankruptcy. The only time you would ever *want to* file bankruptcy, in my opinion, is if you get sued. But even then, it's not the end of the world.

No matter what happens, you have options. You can still settle it with favorable terms, or you can hire an attorney. There are a lot of attorneys who will take your case pro bono. There are nonprofit groups that will help you. They may try to send you something in the mail, but that doesn't count as proof of service.

So, let's assume you do get sued. If you show up in court and plead your case to a judge, in most cases, they tend to be very lenient and are pro-consumer. As I said earlier, they will pretty much tell the two parties, "You two go out in the hallway and figure this out and come back and tell me what your resolution is. If you can't, I am going to come up with one that neither of you will like." Essentially, the stain of bankruptcy follows you in perpetuity. It doesn't even stop after five or ten years.

Most of the time, people in debt will choose bankruptcy because it seems like it will be a quick fix, but that quick fix is momentary because it produces a recovery period that is sometimes more painful to endure than the stress that led to filing bankruptcy in the first place. It is a serious decision that requires much consideration.

Other people decide to tackle their debt themselves. In the next chapter, we'll look inside debt settlement and debt collection departments to better understand the people involved and what will be required of you should you decide to settle your debt on your own.

WHAT YOU CAN DO RIGHT NOW

- If you're considering bankruptcy, you need to understand the differences between a Chapter 13 bankruptcy and a Chapter 7 bankruptcy.
- Since the largest portion of bankruptcies are Chapter 13, consider whether you'll be okay with having all your income and purchases monitored by a trustee for five to seven years.

CHAPTER NINE

SO, YOU THINK YOU WANT TO SETTLE YOUR OWN DEBT?

Would you ever think about building a house without a licensed builder? Would you put in a pool in the backyard without knowing the neighborhood restrictions? Well, you would if you were astutely familiar with the intricacies of that type of work. It wouldn't be the best idea if you had never been a contractor or worked closely with a contractor.

The same goes with the handling your own debt problems. If you asked any one of my colleagues whether you should try to settle your own debt, they would say, "Yeah, you can do it yourself if you love collectors berating you. Have another heaping scoop of that! And if you love getting on the phone and trying to negotiate with someone who doesn't have your best interest in mind, get after it!"

If you thoroughly understand the credit life cycle—the best time to present a settlement offer—go for it. If you understand that speaking with a third-party collector is very different than negotiating with a debt buyer or first-party creditor, give it a whirl!

If you are armed with all the information you need, you don't have to pay someone else to do it. But keep in mind, you don't have the same relationships that debt settlement companies have with collectors, debt buyers, and creditors who have defined strategies around liquidating their portfolios by identifying accounts. You don't have close relationships with your creditors like the counseling companies that can lower your interest rates for a period of time. And you most certainly cannot absolve yourself of all of your debts just because you don't want to or can't pay them anymore.

So, if you fall under any of these categories:

- Your debt is too far out of your control, and you're too close to it to be unemotional in negotiations.
- You take the debt personally and won't get the best outcome for yourself because you think you deserve to be punished.
- You feel like the debt holder won't settle with you at all, and you need the power that a large company has.
- You're unorganized or are too busy, or your debt situation is more complex than you can handle.

. . . you may want to consider getting help from a professional. Sometimes, hiring yourself as the expert isn't always a good idea.

INSIDE A DEBT SETTLEMENT DEPARTMENT

There are lots of creditors, debt buyers, and collection agencies who understand the volume of the accounts sitting in debt settlement. They work very hard to scrub their collection files to identify those accounts that are enrolled with those companies, and they move that segment of the portfolio into a different group that has a one-to-one relationship with those companies that have a defined strategy, which has a collection floor much lower than the general collection floor.

In other words, you might have collectors on the floor who might have the authority to settle accounts at 65% or 70% of the current balance. But if they want to do something below that, they don't have the authority to do it on their own. They have to go to a manager and build a case for why they want to accept an offer less than their defined "floor," and then, they must get the manager to sign off on it.

The debt settlement group in these agencies, as well as debt buying groups and creditors, understand that the current balance on the account is always different from the enrolled balance at the debt settlement company. They also understand that the debt settlement company is always calculating the value of the settlement based on the enrolled balance at the time the consumer entered the program and not what the current balance has grown to with interest, penalties, and fees that have accrued over the pre-charge-off life cycle, which means your balance continues to grow until it is charged off.

Once the account charges off, it no longer accrues interest. It is then a fixed balance. It is a charged-off debt. It then leaves one P&L (profit and loss statement or account) in the bank or creditor and generally goes to another P&L that has a different group with a different set of guidelines for liquidating the debt in that portfolio.

Those are two separate groups within a bank—usually two separate P&Ls. And they have different financial accounting responsibilities, goals, and liquidation targets.

THE DEBT LIFE CYCLE IS ONE TRICKY PUZZLE

Let's say you are a consumer with seven credit cards with $10,000 on each card. You are making your minimum payment every month, but your balance isn't going down. You realize that you are never going to make any progress given where you are. You decide you don't want to file bankruptcy because you won't qualify. Perhaps you have too many assets, which will require you to sell assets and take the proceeds to pay down the debt. Or you know bankruptcy would trash your credit report, which would be detrimental to your job and your ability to function for the next ten years. So now, you are going to settle your debt.

In debt settlement, you are shifting your own money around. If you make $10,000 a month in minimum payments across your credit cards, you need to make that money count. Don't give that money in the form of a minimum payment to satisfy interest to the credit card company every month. Instead, you might move that money into a savings account and keep depositing that every month; all the while, those credit card accounts are becoming delinquent and are getting closer to charge-off, and the value of those accounts is becoming less and less over time. Remember, the more the account becomes delinquent, the less collectible it becomes.

So, when you get to months four and five, the likelihood that the account is going to charge off and become even more uncollectible grows substantially. And by the time that account charges off, its value in the secondary market is somewhere between fifteen to twenty cents on the dollar if the bank wants to sell the account to someone outright.

There is a myriad of factors that impact the value of that account, but to give you a wider range, it is somewhere between ten to twenty cents on the face value of the debt, which includes all the accrued interest up to the date of charge-off.

A debt settlement company doesn't care that the balance grew by $20,000 over those six months. When a consumer enrolls with them, the balance at that time is the balance they are going to negotiate with.

So, when you get into this negotiation on your own behalf, remember that the bank is always working off the latest balance of the debt, which includes interest, penalties, fees, and everything else. And as you know, interest accrues every month and compounds daily. The balance grows. More interest gets charged over six months.

The balance can grow substantially with no payments. If the bank says they will settle your debt for seventy cents on the dollar, that balance to the debt settlement company is really not seventy cents on the dollar because they are working off of a much higher balance, and the debt settlement company is working off a much lower balance.

I know that's a lot of numbers, but I gave that example to introduce a few important pieces to a massive puzzle. Truthfully, as a consumer, if you don't understand how the debt life cycle works and you don't understand that the very same bank willing to do a seventy-cent settlement off your current balance with all the accrued interest, penalties, and fees will settle that very same account with a debt settlement group at the same bank for forty to forty-five cents on the dollar, you aren't going to get very far in settling your own debt.

Could you negotiate the same percentage that a debt settlement company could? That's very unlikely because the person who is doing the negotiation at the bank or collection agency a) doesn't often have the authority to settle debts that deep, and b) when they look at you as a consumer, they look at you like any other potentially naive consumer out there.

They see you are not enrolled in a debt settlement program, so they will automatically assume they are working with an *uneducated consumer*. And they know that most consumers have a deep emotional involvement in the transaction, so they will exploit that to their advantage at every turn.

A DEBT COLLECTOR'S GOAL IS TO MAKE MONEY WHILE SEPARATING YOU FROM YOURS

The goal of a debt collector is to separate you from as much of your money as possible to make the pain stop. It is also to make it as painful as possible up to the limits allowed by law and then get as much money as they possibly can to stop that pain. They use fear, intimidation, shame, guilt, and everything else in their repertoire to put you into a situation where you will pay out everything you possibly can to make it go away. That is their job, and yes, they also get a percentage.

Generally, a debt collector on fresh delinquency (thirty days, sixty days) will get a recovery percentage of 7% to 10% if they can cure the account and bring it current. So, if it takes $500, they will get 10% of that or $50 for the effort.

As time goes on, as the debt becomes more delinquent and the balance becomes less collectible, that number goes up to the point where, in post-charge-off recovery (after the account has been charged off by the bank and it moves into the different P&L), that bank might pay 35% or 40% to a collection agency to recover 60% or 70% of the balance.

Let's say you've got a $10,000 balance. The bank may decide to ride down the balance a little bit. They'll say you owe them $10,000, but they'll take $6,500. Out of that $6,500, the debt collection company gets to keep 30%, 35%, or even 40% of that $6,500, and the rest goes back to the bank.

Even the individual customer service rep gets a percentage. They have a quota of money they have to collect every month, and they are paid a percentage of the collection up to that quota amount. Once they exceed their quota, they are incented at a higher level with a higher percentage they can recover on every dollar they bring in. They also get a bonus based on monthly, quarterly, and annual performance over and above their quota requirements.

As I said before, *everyone's goal is to make money off of you.*

By now, I am sure you are wondering what your chances are for striking a deal. Since those people must have a beating heart, would they ever want to help you out and maybe give you a break?

It depends. You are dealing with a human debt collector who has a personal incentive, and you don't know what that incentive is. It can depend on when you are dealing with that collector—the time of the month, the time of the quarter, and so many other factors you will never know.

In that way, bargaining your own debt payments is much like buying a car. If you go to a car dealership on the next to the last day of the month, you will have a much better opportunity to negotiate a better deal than if you go on the first day of the month.

On the next to the last day of any given month, that car dealer is in "bonus" territory. Either they have made their quota or they haven't, so they are looking for a deal to push them over the line, or they are looking for a deal to push them into the next bonus category. They are more likely to make a deal, depending on what is personally going to benefit them within their compensation plan.

With debt collection, it is no different.

Generally, it is not the last day of the month because that is closing day, and payments usually don't get processed on the same day. But, in the *last week* of the month, you generally have a better chance to negotiate based on those factors.

The point is, when you are dealing with a human who is personally incented to separate you from as many of your dollars as possible, they don't care much about your situation. They won't want to spend a lot of time on the phone chatting with you, trying to negotiate something that is going to fit into their goals and into your budget.

Instead, it is "churn and burn" or "smile and dial." They've got to keep the phones going and the collection queue running. They've got to keep the money coming in. If they don't do that, and they miss their goals and budget, that screws them up for the whole quarter or the whole year.

Well, that's great, you might think. *How does any of this help me save money while paying down my debt? I don't give a rat's ass about a debt collector's monthly quota. I care about getting out of debt!*

And that's exactly my next point. With a solid strategy, you can help others—yes, even debt collectors—while helping yourself.

DEBT VALIDATION

If you have something showing up on your credit file, even if it **is** yours, you can say, "I want this removed." Your goal is to dispute the amount you owe by sending a letter of validation to the collection agency or whoever is listed on your credit report as holding that debt. Your letter might say, "I don't think this debt is mine. You need to prove it is mine." Then the creditor has to supply documentation to prove the debt belongs to you.

That presents a challenge for credit card companies because everything is done online now with electronic signatures. They must prove that you have charges on your card and have copies of the charges. While the creditor might have it, they have to go back and find it. By the time it gets to the collection company, they might not have passed that information along. This starts the clock because now you're trying to validate from the collection company. Some don't want to mess with it, and they just write off the debt right there, just like that. That is the goal of debt validation—get them to write it off so you owe nothing.

That is one of those things that sounds too good to be true **but is actually true** due to the chaos of the creditor hierarchy. There are several parties involved in the process, beginning with the original creditor. Let's say the original creditor doesn't sell the debt, and they use a third-party collection agency to try and collect on it. This third party may or may not have adequate information to challenge your dispute. In turn, they might go back to the bank to ask for help. If the bank doesn't have it, you're more likely to get your debt cleared. If it's too much of a runaround to acquire the proof they need to make your case, chances are they'll just let you off the hook and move on to the next guy.

There are entire companies that handle only debt validation. It begins with the debt validation consultant sending a letter to the collection agency. More often than not, the agency will respond with inadequate documentation. They'll go back and forth a few times, spinning their wheels, making no progress. Often it is a long process that only works if your account has been passed along through multiple collection agencies and they were not able to keep records of the original signed agreement and all purchases. The debt cancellation is what makes it worth it for the consumer to make the phone call. It can be done without a lawyer, but most people do not feel comfortable doing it themselves or hassling with all of the correspondence required.

A DEFINED DEBT STRATEGY

With a defined debt settlement strategy, you are generally working with a group or an individual within the company who has the responsibility to work with those companies and bulk settle as many of the accounts as they can (meaning, they are trading spreadsheets of data). They often present 250 accounts they know are in one particular debt settlement company that they are trying to collect on, and they will put in their settlement offers on those accounts for a lump-sum term settlement. They are doing a lot of the work in large batches, which means they are grouping all of the consumers from one debt settlement company as a whole.

Rather than having one debt collector and one consumer talking on the phone and beating each other up, you have one person at the collection agency dealing with one person at a debt settlement company who is trying to resolve one hundred accounts simultaneously.

There are instances where people at the debt settlement company call debt collectors, banks, or personal loan companies where they don't have a personal relationship or a defined debt settlement strategy, and they have to do one-on-one negotiation. Sometimes you do have these one-off communications with debt settlement companies and debt collectors, either at the bank or an agency. But when you have those discussions, all the emotion is taken out of it because you have a third-party intermediary between the consumer and the debt collection agency.

You've basically declawed the debt collector at that point. The debt collector knows that there is no amount of coercion or threat or intimidation they can use or invoke during the conversation to get someone to act because the person they are dealing with doesn't have an ounce of skin in the game. If they don't reach a settlement, that person will hang up the phone, go to the next account in the queue, call the next debt collector, and work on the next settlement.

That will happen fifty times that day, and they are not going to lose an ounce of sleep over it. So, you take all the emotional attachment out of it. You are eliminating any sort of fear, threat, and lack of knowledge because those people understand how the debt is supposed to settle.

The debt settlement companies themselves have certain parameters under which they can settle debt. So, like a bank, the debt settlement company will not take a settlement for 85% of the current balance of the debt. After the consumer pays the fee, that is more than they would have paid the debt collector. Instead, when a company realizes that a third-party intermediary is involved in the process and there is a legal structure in place—basically a "Cease and Desist" from the consumer authorizing an agent to speak on their behalf—most people, at that point, will agree to it and deal with the debt settlement company.

Again, the point of going into all this detail about the settlement cycle is just to say that your true mission should be to find an expert, and if that expert is you, and you have all the tools to get your debt settled for the least amount of money, by all means, give it your very best shot.

STEP 1: GETTING YOUR MIND RIGHT FOR THE FIGHT

Your first hurdle in the "do it yourself" scenario will be your mindset. You have to get your mind right. I mention it over and over in this book for a reason—it is one of the most important things you can do.

No one talks about the psychology of the debt. When you find yourself unable to pay the debt you owe, you might feel like a deadbeat. "Deadbeat" is the term creditors use for you when you miss payments. It's harsh. They want to make you feel like a deadbeat to guilt you into paying. But if you understand the relationship created in the beginning, that we all get sucked into the game we ultimately have to play to get the credit score we need, you will be able to take back the reins of control. You almost have to step outside of yourself, relinquish the personal feelings of guilt and shame, and treat yourself as if you were a business.

Think about what a business would do if they got into debt trouble. I can tell you what they would do. They would start restructuring their debt. As a consumer, you need to be able to restructure your debt so you can get yourself out of the situation. People under duress while making financial decisions will tend to make poorer financial decisions because they are just not thinking well.

And who is going to call you when the problem starts? Your unsecured creditors. They are going to apply pressure, and you may do something impulsive like make a payment to an unsecured credit card instead of your car, which you need to get around in. Now, you are upside down with the car; the car gets repossessed, which leads to not getting to work and losing your job. In getting your mind right, you need to know that every move you make has a consequence.

STEP 2: MANAGING MULTIPLE CREDITORS

The second step is recognizing exactly what you are in for. You will be managing multiple creditors and prioritizing who gets what, and that is a lot of hard work. You will need to determine what you owe, decide on a reasonable timeframe to accumulate enough money to settle with each of your creditors, and then save that amount month in and month out.

Can you liquidate any assets to contribute to that savings? If so, you need to talk to your creditors, *all* your creditors, probing and playing the game. Which one of your creditors will be the first one you can strike a deal with? Once you have that deal in place, will that allow you to have enough left to work out another deal with another creditor?

Another challenge you will run into is calling your creditor and hearing, "There is nothing I can do for you." That goes back to you calling that 800 number. And we are all taught to do the right thing. When we see a problem coming, we try to be proactive and work something out with the creditors. That *is* the right thing to do. But sometimes, the person on the other end of the line says, "I don't even know what you are talking about. All I see on my screen is you are current. There is nothing I can do for you."

DAVE'S DEBT SNOWBALL

Dave Ramsey's "debt snowball" is a useful method to incorporate at this point to determine which creditors to pay first. Simply make a list of your balances, smallest at the top, largest at the bottom. Then, moving down from the top, send money to the creditor with the smallest balance while you keep paying minimum payments to each of the rest of the creditors on the list. Then, save up enough money to pay the next smallest balance on the list.

The "snowball" effect is that as you pay each balance off, you will be able to add the money you were saving for that particular payment to the next smallest balance. You never have to come up with *more money* as you go along. You are taking that same amount and applying it and applying it . . . snowball. And it works. If you are at a certain level, have enough income, and can afford to cut back or just apply more, it's a smart way to go. You will be surprised at the momentum you gather, paying your creditors this way.

Ramsey knows that most people get into problems because they subconsciously lose an attachment to their money. Therefore, they lose the perception of the value of their money, and they don't have a defined strategy or set of goals to get back to a healthy place with it. Essentially, they have a poor relationship with money. The way to reprogram people to have a better relationship with their money is to start with very small, very defined practices repeated over a twenty to forty-day cycle.

What he is talking about is to get the consumer out of their unconscious negative actions that have destroyed their relationship with money and finances, have them be aware that money has worked against them because of those practices, and then retrain them to do things to put them in a position to make money work for them in a positive way. He also makes it clear that income is the greatest tool you have to reduce your debt. That is 100% true.

Most people can't raise the thermostat high enough or cut the shopping budget low enough to make an impact. So, it is either take the self-sacrifice route where you have to be willing to eat three meals a week for a family of four that costs $5 or less to produce (which is a pot of beans, rice, and cornbread) or you have to be able to substantially increase your income. People who use the Ramsey strategy of paying off debt usually have the financial means to do so. They are really not *distressed* consumers in most cases. They are simply people who haven't developed good financial habits yet.

The only problem with the debt snowball is not the methodology at all—it is the consumer. In my experience, I have found that people (myself included) don't like to sacrifice if they don't have to. They don't want to give up their Starbucks. They want the least pain and friction possible. They don't want to deal with the harassing phone calls every day on top of the stress they are already feeling about the unpaid debt.

POSITIVES OF DOING IT YOURSELF

It saves you money (unless it doesn't). It is true that you will pay fees to a debt settlement company. Usually, their pitch is that they will settle your debt for about half of what you owe. That is true. It is also true that they will charge about 20% of what you owe in fees. In the end, you get about a 30% break on your debt. So, a DIY approach will save you that 20% you would be paying in fees, but you need to know that the 20% is going somewhere. Now, it is going to *you*. You will be spending your time and energy researching and talking with your creditors. They all have different policies when it comes to settling debt. Some creditors don't settle debt until it is at least ninety days old, while others will not settle debt at all, and you have to wait it out until the debt gets sold to a third party. Some creditors are more likely to sue than others. You need to be armed with all that information before you make any offers because making an offer to the wrong creditor first or at the wrong time could cost you more than doing it yourself saves you.

It saves you time (unless it doesn't). It may take a debt settlement company two to six months to settle your debt. You could possibly get faster results by using a DIY approach. The problem is that negotiating a settlement on your own is only a good option if your account is at least ninety days late already and works even better when you are five or six months behind.

The problem with that is you will undoubtedly be hit with late fees and penalties, your credit score will take a big hit, you may be sent to a collection agency, and you may get your wages garnished.

NEGATIVES OF DOING IT YOURSELF

You will probably have to go over your story several times with several different people. As you can imagine, banks are huge. You could call in a hundred different times and talk to a hundred different people. Sometimes, you have to dig in and find that specific personality who will listen to you plead your case. If you don't hear what you like the first time, hang up, call back, and talk to another person.

Settling your debt will become your part-time job. By the time you have decided to search out ways to settle your debt, you are probably already overwhelmed with your situation. You may have even tried to call your bank and were told there was nothing they could do because you are still what they consider "current" when they pull your account up on their screen.

Lack of education and experience. This goes back to hiring an expert if you want the very best outcome. Your creditors have quarterly profits they have to hit, and they will adjust their needs accordingly. The end of the month is an example when, in collections, you'll find creditors to be more lenient.

It happens every month, and especially every quarter, when someone on high calls their servicing agents and says, "We need to hit our numbers" or "We need to exceed our numbers, so loosen up." Suddenly, those who had a settlement authority at 65% can now settle at 30%. They'll do it for a short time, and then they are back to business as usual.

People with experience in this industry know the appropriate time to hit that sweet spot when dealing with creditors, whereas the average consumer will not.

The harassing phone calls from creditors don't stop. The sound of the phone ringing at this point makes your blood pressure spike, and a sense of dread comes over you. You have to prepare yourself to go through months of these relentless phone calls and demeaning rhetoric.

In the process of trying to save money, you may lose money. Creditors do not get their money while saving yours. They are skilled negotiators and quite often talk you into a settlement that costs you money instead of saving you money.

HOW DO I KNOW IF I SHOULD TRY TO SETTLE MY OWN DEBT?

The discussion we have been having here is—should you hire someone to do this who has the knowledge, expertise, resources, and experience? Or do you try to save that 20% and do it yourself?

The question is often if you hire an agency to do it, can they settle your debt at a lower level to offset their fee? Even if they can't drop it the full 20%, there is an intangible value of your time, sanity, and stress level by not having to deal with this incredibly difficult and stressful process yourself.

I used an example with the regulator at the CFPB (Consumer Financial Protection Bureau) one day. I was having a discussion with the person in charge of writing the laws for enforcement, and they said, "Every consumer out there can settle their own debt. They have the same options available to them that every debt settlement company has."

I said, "No, that is not exactly the case because you and I both know that anyone who has a defined strategy around debt settlement has a different settlement authority than the base collection settlement authority on the floor for a debt collector."

He said, "Yeah, but they can go around that and get a supervisor to review a hardship, and there are programs for that."

I said, "Yeah, if the consumer is sophisticated and educated and knows about those programs." There was silence. "You guys always talk about the least sophisticated consumer. How many of those consumers actually know how the system works and can settle their debt with a point of advantage in their favor?"

"Well, okay, I'll concede that point," he said.

Sometimes, it simply pays in more ways than one to use professionals.

For example, I can clean my own house. I have a vacuum cleaner and a closet full of cleaning supplies. It takes me six, seven, eight hours to clean my house from top to bottom. But I can pay $200 to a professional cleaning service to clean my house in two hours. Every picture frame is dusted, every fan blade cleaned, every cabinet face wiped down—everything.

Now, I bill my clients a certain amount of money an hour. So, what is the value of that four to six hours of my time that I couldn't bill for my services? There is a cost-benefit analysis that people have to do on this. It is never as simple as it is made out to be. Just because someone *can* do it themselves doesn't mean they *should* do it themselves.

Everyone has a certain level of tolerance for what they are willing to go through. Everyone has a certain skill set. There are always pros and cons. You need to make an honest assessment based on your personality, circumstances, ability, willingness to put up with the pain—all of that. If it is worth it to you to outsource all that to an expert who has defined relationships and has demonstrated success in this area, that might be a good choice for you. If you want to go slug it out, you think you can do a great job of it, and you are disciplined enough to stop spending and start putting money into a savings account (because you are going to have to have a war chest to do this), the DIY path may be right for you.

Part of it is discipline. Part of it is ability. Part of it is just your own peace of mind and how much you are willing to go through to do it yourself.

A key piece of deciding whether or not to settle your own debt is arming yourself with as much knowledge as possible. In the next chapter, we'll explain how the credit industry works and what you need to know about your rights as a consumer.

WHAT YOU CAN DO RIGHT NOW

- Ready to settle your own debt? Take a moment to ask yourself these questions: Can you be unemotional in negotiations? Do you take the debt personally, or can you distance yourself from it and not feel as though you deserve to be punished for having the debt?
- Remember that *everyone's goal is to make money off of you*. Studying the debt life cycle will help you understand how essential timing can be to debt negotiations and repayment.
- Create your own defined debt strategy to ensure you know all of your financial details so you can keep track of all communication with your creditors.

CHAPTER TEN

KNOWLEDGE IS POWER

Dealing with a Credit Setback
with Mark A. Carey, Esq.

One of the most important educational goals of this book—and for you as a consumer—is to be knowledgeable about your rights.

We all know the adage that "knowledge is power," but let's take it even further. The power comes from the application of that knowledge, and the most power comes from the correct application of the correct knowledge. Any knowledge we have is useless as a defensive or offensive weapon if we don't know how to use it.

The truth is that when it comes to banks and credit, you are a cog in the wheel. Unfortunately, you are a very small cog, and most of the power belongs to the Big Wheels—the banks and credit lenders—who write the rules. But just because you are a small cog doesn't mean you are powerless. It does not mean you have no rights. And it does not mean you are alone in your struggles.

Let's start with some statistics that might make you feel a bit better. Remember when I said you are not alone? You aren't. The latest census data for the United States shows that there are just over 209 million people over the age of eighteen. As of 2018, there were more than 1.1 trillion credit cards (that is a one with twelve zeroes after it—1,000,000,000,000). Think about that. There are nearly five times more credit cards being used in the United States than there are Americans over the age of eighteen. Not surprisingly, those same statistics show that the average American adult has four credit cards.

As of 2019, there are approximately sixty-eight million Americans with at least one credit card account in collections. That means sixty-eight million of your fellow citizens are currently in collections. I bring up these statistics so that you do not feel alone—as if you are the only person who is struggling with debt. In all likelihood, several of your friends, coworkers, or neighbors are in the very same situation you are in. Your situation is happening to *millions* of others, even as you read this.

I am not saying the banks and lenders want you to fail and go into collections. But understand that the banks already knew that a certain percentage of those they extended credit to *would* go into collections. Banks write the rules and credit agreements to ensure that they make money no matter what happens. Late fees, charges, and increased interest rates if you miss a payment are all designed to ensure the bank is paid and to maximize its profit off of you.

BANKS WILL MAKE MONEY OFF YOU EITHER WAY

Did you ever notice that for the first ten years or so of your mortgage payments, most of what you pay is interest? That ensures that the bank makes their money off you right away in case something happens to you later in the term of that mortgage loan. So, if you've ever thought the bank was so nice, offering to let you make "interest-only" payments or put you into forbearance for a period of time, you need to change your perspective. It is nice in that it might help you out of a temporary jam, but make no mistake, the bank is making its money back (and then some) the longer you take to pay. Again, let me stress that the bank is not necessarily hoping you go into collections. Just understand that they have prepared for every contingency in case you do to ensure they make money.

Your initial relationship with the bank is similar to a marriage. Each has something the other wants. You want credit extended to you, and the bank wants the interest payments (the profit) they will make for extending that credit to you. (The bank makes money off of you in ways you don't even realize, but that's a story for a different chapter!)

You enter into a contract with the bank wherein they loan you the money and you promise to pay it back. You are then in the honeymoon phase—you got your credit and bought that car you were coveting, and every month, you paid the bank your agreed-upon amount. Everyone is happy. But then, an event or series of events occurs, and your relationship with the bank changes. You lose your job. A family member has an unforeseen medical emergency. Your spouse leaves you, and you have only one income with which to pay your bills. Whatever the reason, you can't pay your utilities, food bills, put gas in your car to get to work, and pay the bank, so you miss your payment. You are unwittingly in the jaws of the trap, and the snowball effect begins.

Next month, your minimum payment has doubled (last month's payment plus the current payment) plus late fees. A missed payment might also trigger a massive hike in your interest rate. If you were unable to make one month's payment, how can you now make two? And how can you pay a 20% interest rate? And so on and so on. Despite your best intentions, you and the bank are about to have your first argument and may be headed for divorce. The issue now is determining who gets custody of the money and how they get that custody.

Regardless of how you might feel, it is not personal. You are not a bad person. I cannot stress that strongly enough. I have sat across from hundreds of people in your position who all tell me something similar: They feel horrible. Their self-esteem has taken a blow. For perhaps the first time in their lives, they are unable to pay their debts. It can be a very unsettling blow to one's ego and sense of self-worth. But most of you know that if there were a way you could live up to your obligations, you would.

So, take a deep breath. The event that put you in your current situation has already occurred. There's nothing you can do about the past, so it's best to look ahead and take the next steps toward a solution.

You are probably getting letters and telephone calls asking you, "Where is my money?" If so, you are likely thinking, *There is nothing I can do. I borrowed the money, and I did promise to pay. But I cannot control this situation.*

Or can you?

I say you can, with the right knowledge and the right application of the right knowledge.

There are several governmental agencies, including the Consumer Financial Protection Bureau (CFPB) and the Federal Trade Commission (FTC), whose job it is to oversee the banking and credit industry to make sure that you, the small cog, the consumer, does not get taken advantage of by the Big Wheels merely because they wrote the rules.

Those governmental agencies have put into place certain federal statutes designed to help protect you as you go through the divorce process with your bank or lending institution. To see if those agencies and the rules and regulations they have put in place will help you, we must first determine who is contacting or calling you—the original creditor or a third-party creditor?

FIRST-PARTY CREDITOR (THE ORIGINAL CREDITOR)

A first-party or original creditor is the bank or other lending institution that loaned you the money or extended the credit to you.

Here's a simple example. You walk into a bank and apply for a car loan. The loan is given to you. The loan agreement is between you and the bank, and you are both first parties to that agreement. No one else is part of that agreement. In this example, the bank is the original creditor.

Here's a slightly trickier example. You apply for a Visa card online and it is approved. The bank or lending institution providing that money is the original creditor. (Visa is not the creditor; there is a bank behind the card supplying the credit. Visa is just the trade name of the card company that facilitates the engagement and processes transactions.) The credit agreement is between you and the bank. Just like the example above, you and the bank are both parties to the agreement. No one else is part of that agreement.

THIRD-PARTY CREDITOR (A COLLECTION AGENCY)

A third-party creditor is a person or entity—usually a collection agency—who was *not* a party to your agreement with the bank. You never did business with them and have no agreement with them. You are left wondering, *If I didn't have an agreement with them, how did the collection agency get my information? Why are they calling me and not the bank?* Here is how it works.

Let's continue with the Visa example from above. You begin using your new Visa card, and every month, you make your minimum monthly payments. Keep in mind that the banks want you to make the minimum payment *only* because they make more in interest! (A relatively new law now requires that credit card companies include on the monthly statement how long it will take to pay and how much extra you will spend if you make *only* minimum payments. Take a look. It will shock you!)

The event—whatever it was—that prevented you from making that payment happens. After missing a payment or two, you start to get calls from the bank. They'll be polite at first. "Hello, sir. This is the bank calling about your credit card. Looks like you forgot to make your last payment."

Now, of course, you didn't forget! The bank just doesn't want to come out and ask, "Where's my money?" But let's say they call and try to get their money from you for three months, to no avail. You just don't have it, so you can't possibly pay it. At that point, the bank decides they are losing money by paying their employees to spend time and effort to collect a debt that is simply not collectible at that time. The bank then makes a business decision (remember, this is not personal) and takes your debt, along with the debts of thousands of other people who, just like you, have an uncollectible debt, and closes the accounts, marking them as "charged-off." Those debts are then placed into a special file or portfolio. For our purposes here, we will call it the "Bad Debt" portfolio.

The bank then does one of two things:

1. They send the Bad Debt portfolio to a collection agency that will attempt to collect the debt from you. (Remember? A collection agency is a third party with whom you have no prior relationship and is not part of the original agreement.) In this scenario, the collection agency gets paid a percentage of what they collect, and only if they collect from you, or

2. The bank sells the entire Bad Debt portfolio to a debt buyer for a percentage of the face value of the debts owed, often pennies on the dollar, who will then assign the right to collect that debt to a collection agency. Under either scenario, your debt is in the hands of a third-party debt collector. The rules now change slightly in your favor.

That is why the distinction between original and third-party creditor is so important. Whereas an original creditor, the bank, can call you and say or do pretty much what they want to get their money, a third party cannot. If you think about it, that makes a certain amount of sense. The money is the bank's money, and they are entitled to it. However, a third party is collecting someone else's money (the bank's money) and is bound by certain laws and rules they must follow while attempting to collect money from you.

So, let's say the calls are coming from a collection agency. You have spoken to them several times and have explained (often in painstaking and demoralizing detail) the very personal situation you find yourself in that prevents you from fulfilling your obligations. It's humiliating. Degrading. You are stressed and anxious. The phone keeps ringing, and you know it's them, but you feel as though you cannot explain it to yet another collector, so you don't answer, which in turn prompts more calls, causing you more stress and anxiety. Just like your monthly payments, the vicious collection cycle snowballs. The calls increase, and so does the pressure on you.

Given that hundreds of thousands of collection calls occur daily, it is safe to say that only a small percentage of the calls violate the law. To that point, the mere fact that a collection agency is calling you is, in most circumstances, legal. Debt collection agencies are allowed to call you. It's the job they were hired to do, and most do it lawfully. But, sometimes, debt collectors cross a line.

HOW DEBT COLLECTION AGENCIES WORK

As we discussed earlier, the collection agency often collects the debts assigned to it on a contingency fee basis. That means the agency does not get paid unless and until you pay. The debt collectors who work for the agency also get paid—partially—and on a contingency basis. The collectors make an hourly wage, but their real incentive is the bonuses they will receive based on how much they collect. The more they collect, the more they make. There is a huge monetary incentive for those collectors to push you hard to pay on your account. The collector wants to make as much money as they can. There is nothing wrong with that. Don't we all want to maximize our income?

But sometimes, that desire to make money causes the collector to use bad judgment and act illegally. Perhaps they are short of the amount needed to make bonus that month. So, they decide to push the envelope a bit—go beyond what they are allowed to do or say—in an effort to get in a payment that will get them to their goal. Sometimes it isn't simply greed that drives them to cross a boundary. Sometimes they are about to lose their job if they can't bring in a certain amount of money, and that pressure causes them to act illegally. Whatever the reason, it is never pleasant to be on the receiving end of an illegal call.

One of the laws designed to protect you is the Fair Debt Collection Practices Act (FDCPA). The very first line states, "There is abundant evidence of the use of abusive, deceptive, and unfair debt collection practices by many debt collectors." In other words, collection abuses got so bad that way back in 1977–78, Congress felt the need to step in and create a law designed to help protect you from abusive debt collection practices.

The FDCPA provides a list of things a debt collector cannot do when attempting to collect a debt from you. The list includes things that are considered abusive, deceptive, or unfair, including (but not limited to):

- Asking you to pay more than you owe.
- Asking you to pay interest, fees, or expenses that are not allowed by law or by the original agreement.
- Calling repeatedly or continuously.
- Using obscene, profane, or abusive language.
- Calling before 8:00 a.m. or after 9:00 p.m.
- Calling at times the collector knows or should know are inconvenient (like while at work after you have told them not to call you during your working hours).
- Using or threatening to use violence if you don't pay the debt.
- Threatening action they cannot or will not take, such as filing a lawsuit when they are not a law firm, or the debt is outside the Statute of Limitations.
- Telling anyone else (except your lawyer or spouse) about your debt.
- Repeatedly calling a third party to try and get your location information even after that third party tells them they don't know how to contact you.
- Contacting you at work.
- Failing to send a written debt validation notice.
- Ignoring your written request to verify the debt and continue to collect.
- Continuing to collect on the debt before providing verification.
- Continuing collection attempts after receiving a cease communication notice.

The law also sets out what a debt collection agency is liable for if they break it:

- Statutory damages not exceeding $1,000. The FDCPA is known as a "*per se*" statute, which means you are entitled to up to $1,000 even if you have not sustained any other actual damages. (You are entitled to up to $1,000 per case, not per violation. If a debt collector violates three different parts of the statute, you are entitled to a total of up to $1,000, not $3,000.)
- Actual damages sustained *as a direct result* of the collector's illegal actions (things such as lost wages, stress, anxiety, humiliation, medical expenses, etc.).
- The costs of the action (court costs).
- Reasonable attorney fees.

The collection agency that violates the law is obligated to pay you those sums. It is designed to discourage the collector or creditor from continuing to engage in abusive, deceptive, and unfair conduct.

How do you know if your rights have been violated? A consumer can read the statute and think, *Oh! They called, and they were abusive or mean to me. I have a claim!* But a word of caution here. What you might believe to be abusive could be completely legal.

HOW TO KNOW WHEN YOUR RIGHTS HAVE BEEN VIOLATED

So, again, how do you know if your rights have been violated? The short answer is *you don't*. Even knowing the law is not enough if you do not know how that law is applied. (Remember our mantra—we need the right knowledge plus the right application of the right knowledge.) These cases are very fact-specific and can be won or lost on a technicality. To make it even more complex, different courts in different states have interpreted the rules and laws differently.

Some examples of illegal activity are easy to spot:

- The collector gets rude, mean, or argumentative. "Hey, don't be a deadbeat; just pay your bills!" "Why do you make us keep calling you when you owe the debt. Just pay!"

- The collector threatens you with something bad, either today or soon, if you don't pay. "If I can't get a down payment of at least $500 today, I am going to have to report this to the police." "We are going to have the sheriff out there this afternoon to take your car if you can't pay us today."

But most other examples are far more subtle and difficult to recognize, especially for consumers like yourself!

To illustrate how technical this can be, let's take the following set of facts and demonstrate how even a small change to those facts can make a phone call go from legal to illegal.

FACTS: YOUR ACCOUNT IS CURRENTLY IN COLLECTIONS.

When you applied for your loan with the bank, you listed your cell phone number as your contact number. You also provided your employer's name, address, and telephone number as part of your loan application so the bank could verify your employment and assess your creditworthiness.

Scenario 1: The debt collector calls you on your cell phone during work hours. Your boss, upset with you for taking personal calls while at work, fires you! Horrible, right? Yes. But is what the collector did illegal? No. The debt collector has the right to contact you at the number you provided as a contact number on your loan application.

But even slight changes in the facts change the outcome. What if the collector had been told a month earlier not to contact you at work but calls you there anyway? Now the call to you is illegal. You can sue for your statutory damages of up to $1,000, plus you lost your job and have actual damages as well.

Scenario 2: What if the debt collector calls your employer's phone, asks to speak with you about a personal matter, and your boss fires you because you are taking personal calls? Is this illegal? No. You provided your employer's number on the application, and some courts have held that to be tacit permission to call you at that number. Thus, for the same reason as above, the call to that number is probably okay.

But what if the debt collector calls that same work number and says, "I am calling from ABC Collection Agency, and I need to speak with John

Jones (you) about a personal matter." Is that illegal? Yes, because now the debt collector just disclosed to the person who answered the phone, a person other than your spouse or attorney, that you have an account in collections.

One little change made all the difference in determining whether or not your rights were violated.

Scenario 3: Let's assume that the call while at work is okay because it's during your lunch break when you told them to call you, and your boss doesn't mind. During the call with the collector, the collector says, "I would really like to help you with this today. If you can pay just $20 today, it might prevent a negative report on your credit."

Sounds great, doesn't it? Just $20, and you can get off the call. Nothing wrong here, right? As written, no. But what if the debt they call about is out of statute (so old that you cannot be sued for it even if you do owe it)? If that's the case, the call is illegal.

If the debt is out of statute, it cannot be reported to a credit bureau, so the collector's suggestion that this "might prevent a negative report on your credit" is a lie. What's worse, if you did make that $20 payment on a debt that is out of statute, you may have just re-started the statute, and now you can be sued for the debt.

Scenario 4: The call at work happens while you're at lunch, your boss doesn't mind, and the debt is valid, so paying $20 will indeed save a negative report on your credit. But it's Tuesday, and you don't get paid until Friday, so you tell the collector, "Here is my bank or debit card information; just don't debit my account until Friday." But the collector, either innocently or intentionally, debits your account later that day. Legal? No! Even though you gave permission, you gave permission for Friday, not Tuesday.

You are entitled to up to $1,000 for that violation plus any actual damages you might have. You might ask, "What actual damages?" What if taking that money out on Tuesday meant that your automatically withdrawn mortgage payment bounced? Now you have a $35 bounced check fee, a late charge, or worse, another negative "ding" on your credit. The collection agency is liable for that as well.

Sometimes, it is not what the collector says or does, but instead is what they do not say or do. When you receive a collection letter in the mail (known in the industry as a "dunning" letter), that letter must be written with specific language and certain disclosures contained within it. Many states have different or additional disclosures and requirements. If you received a letter not written with the right disclosures, your rights were violated, and you would not even know it.

Similarly, collectors must recite certain disclosures before they even begin to talk to a consumer. For example, one of the things a debt collector must say when they call is, "This is a call from a debt collector and is an attempt to collect a debt. Any information gathered will be used for that purpose." It is a violation *not* to say it, but if you're not familiar with the law, you'd have no way of knowing you were supposed to have information disclosed to you at the start of a call.

You are going to need help to navigate these technicalities.

The whole purpose of these examples is to illustrate just how fine a line it can be between legal and illegal activity. One simple word—or lack of a word—can change the entire situation. Most of the time, the illegal activities are, like the examples above, very difficult to determine.

Most consumers don't do anything when they are being harassed by debt collectors. Like I said earlier, most have no idea that the debt collector's behavior is illegal. Even if a consumer senses that something isn't right, many believe they have to take it as some form of punishment for being unable to meet their financial obligations.

What consumers *should do* is educate themselves. That's what you are doing by reading this book.

If the consumer senses or knows that they are being harassed, the best option is to seek legal help. I don't normally like to advise people to run to a lawyer to solve a problem, but this area of the law, as you saw from the examples above, is so technical and nuanced that you will need the assistance of a lawyer. Not just any lawyer, but a lawyer well versed in handling these types of matters. Just like you don't go to a gastroenterologist for a broken leg, you don't want a personal injury or corporate lawyer to review your case. You need a lawyer who handles consumer rights cases. As a consumer rights attorney, I know the questions to ask *you* to discover whether there's been a violation, but most other types of lawyers won't. Like anything else, the knowledge comes from experience and repetition.

The internet is replete with lawyers who advertise for these types of cases, and while I loathe attorney advertisers, such is the nature of the business. A consumer rights lawyer will review your case for free (if they don't, run!), and if you have a case, they will handle it with no upfront cost to you.

If you are unsure of who to go to, where to turn, or if the lawyer is reputable, reach out to us and we will make sure you get where you need to go! You can find more information here:

Up to now, I have focused this chapter on only one of the statutes—the FDCPA—designed to help protect you. Several other federal statutes are also designed to safeguard your rights, and I will touch on them briefly.

THE FAIR CREDIT REPORTING ACT (FCRA)

Every person who has ever bought anything on credit has a credit history maintained by what is known as a Credit Reporting Agency (CRA). Currently, there are three known to almost everyone: Equifax, Experian, and TransUnion. The law that governs how a CRA and your creditors handle your credit information is called the Fair Credit Reporting Act (FCRA).

A CRA maintains and retains *all* information about each one of your past and present credit transactions. That credit information and history, known as your "credit report," is what is made available to banks or other lenders who want to know if they should extend credit to you.

WHY IS YOUR CREDIT REPORT AND CREDIT SCORE SO IMPORTANT?

A full credit report will show how much credit you have outstanding (how much you currently owe creditors), how much money you have coming in (your income), how much credit you have available to you on each credit card, if you pay your bills on time (if you don't pay on time, it will show how often you are late and for how long you were delinquent or overdue), and if your past accounts were closed or charged-off by the creditor because you didn't pay or if the accounts were closed because you paid them off. A CRA looks at all that information and, based on that information, assigns to you a rating known as your "credit score."

When you apply for a loan, the bank or lender "pulls" your credit report, reviews your credit history and your credit score, and decides if you are creditworthy. "Creditworthiness" is a nice way for the bank to say to themselves, "This consumer wants to borrow our money. Is she worth the risk?" Your credit score and the information in your credit reports seriously affects your ability to qualify for jobs, mortgages, loans, credit cards, and insurance. Your credit score will determine what car you drive, what type of house you live in, and what type of credit card you qualify for. The worse your credit score, the less likely it is you will get the credit. If you get the credit, it will be at a much higher interest rate than that given to someone with a better credit score.

WHAT IS THE FCRA, AND WHAT ARE YOUR RIGHTS UNDER IT?

Now that we know why your credit report and score are so important, let me explain how the FCRA can help you protect your report and your score.

The FCRA is a federal law regulating the use of your consumer credit information. The law applies to the credit reporting agencies that collect information and those who furnish information to them. The purpose of the law is to protect you, the consumer, against inaccurate or out of date information on your credit report. The statute is very long and filled with "legalese," but there are several items that are of interest to everyone concerned about having an accurate credit report.

The FCRA requires you to monitor your own credit. The good news is that you are entitled to one free credit report a year from a CRA. (Sites like CreditKarma.com, FreeCreditReport.com, and others make it easy to obtain that report and your score.)

"So, what do I do if there is an error on my report?"

If you find an error on your credit report, you are allowed to have inaccurate information removed. You must send a dispute letter to the creditor or the CRA (or both) before taking any legal action.

Once a creditor or the CRA receives the letter from you, it must:

1. Conduct a reasonable investigation into your dispute; and
2. Prepare a credit report as accurately and up to date as possible, following all policies and procedures.

If the CRA or the creditor who furnished the credit information to the CRA fails to investigate and correct persistent errors in your credit report, the FCRA gives you the right to fight back. If you follow the required dispute process, the FCRA allows you to sue creditors who do not notify CRAs of your dispute and the CRA that fails to investigate or correct your report in a timely fashion. You can also sue those who report or access your credit reports improperly, like creditors and debt collectors.

COMMON VIOLATIONS OF THE FCRA

Furnishing and Reporting Old Information

Credit Reporting Agencies (CRAs) and those who supply them information (furnishers) are required to keep the information up to date and accurate.

Violations include:

- Failing to report a debt that has been discharged in bankruptcy.
- Reporting credit information that is more than seven years old or ten years for civil judgments.
- Reporting old debts as newer than they are (re-aging).
- Reporting an account as active that was voluntarily closed by the consumer.

Furnishing and Reporting Inaccurate Information
- Reporting a debt as charged-off when it was settled or paid in full
- Misstating the amount due or late payments when payment was not late
- Supplying credit information despite reported identity theft
- Listing you as a debtor on an account where you were only an authorized user

Mixing Files
- Mixing credit information of other people into your credit report

Failing to Follow Debt Dispute Procedures

When you submit a written dispute about the accuracy of items on your report, the credit reporting agencies and furnishers have a duty to conduct a reasonable investigation of your dispute. There are several ways they can fall short of this duty, and then you may have a claim against them for money damages.

Debt Dispute Violations by Credit Reporting Agencies
- Not notifying the creditor that you have disputed the reported debt
- Not conducting a reasonable investigation of your dispute
- Not correcting or deleting inaccurate, incomplete, or unverifiable information within thirty days of receiving your written dispute

Debt Dispute Violations by Creditors and Other Furnishers of Information
- Not notifying every CRA that you dispute the debt
- Not submitting corrected information to the CRA after investigating your dispute
- Continuing to submit information it knows or should know is incorrect
- Not conducting an internal investigation of your dispute within thirty days

- Not providing you with a reasonable procedure to submit your written dispute
- Not informing you of the results of its investigation within five days of its completion of the investigation

Privacy Violations

CRAs can release your credit report *only* to authorized persons. Authorized persons are those with a "valid need." For instance:
- Creditors
- Landlords
- Insurers
- Utilities
- Employers (only if you gave express consent)

Improper Requests for Credit Reports

Authorized persons must have a "permissible purpose" every time they pull your credit report from a CRA. Some examples of impermissible purposes are:
- Your employer pulls a report without your specific permission
- A creditor for a debt discharged in bankruptcy pulls a report after the bankruptcy

Notice Violations

You are entitled by law to a notice of reporting and handling of your credit reports.
- When a creditor reports negative information to a CRA.
- When an authorized person who accesses your report makes a negative decision based on the report.
- A creditor must notify you of your credit score if it was used in its decision.

- A creditor must notify you of your right to dispute inaccurate information and to obtain a free credit report.
- A creditor or authorized person must identify the source of the credit information it obtained on you (Equifax, Experian, or TransUnion).

THE TELEPHONE CONSUMER PROTECTION ACT (TCPA)

The Telephone Consumer Protection Act (TCPA) is a federal statute that prohibits all autodialed or prerecorded calls or text messages to your cell phone. The statute also applies to landlines and fax machines for telemarketing calls, but this chapter focuses on debt collection activities.

DEBT COLLECTION CALLS

Debt collectors are prohibited from making robocalls to your cell phone to collect on a debt unless you have given them specific permission to do so. Debt collectors cannot make a call to your cell phone using an automatic telephone dialing system or using a computer-generated, artificial, or prerecorded voice. They can, however, make nonautomated calls to you even if you have added your name to the Do Not Call List.

SIGNS THAT A CALL IS AN AUTODIALED ROBOCALL

Have you heard clicks or stretches of quiet between the time you answer your phone and when someone comes on the other end of the call?

Have you ever received calls where no one is on the line, so you hang up, but a few seconds later, you get a call from a debt collector?

Have you ever noticed getting calls where the caller says, "Sorry, wrong number" and hangs up, but a few seconds later, you just happen to get a call from a debt collector?

Have you ever gotten a text message from a debt collector? If you didn't give your permission for that text to your cell phone, that might be a violation of the law.

Those are all examples of potential robocalls.

If you receive more than four calls or voicemails a day from the same caller, that is a sign that the caller is using an autodialer.

If you answer a call and hear only a recording or computerized voice, it usually means it is a robocall. If you answer a call and no one speaks, that can also signal that it is a robocall.

WHAT YOU CAN DO TO STOP ROBOCALLS

Revoke Consent If Previously Given

The FCC has determined that you must give written consent for a caller to make robocalls to your cell phone. Unfortunately, listing your cell phone on the credit or loan application is often considered consent to be called at that number. If you have given such consent in the past but have now changed your mind, you can send another letter revoking consent.

If the Calls Are from Telemarketers, Opt Out of Calls from a Specific Caller

The Federal Communications Commission (FCC) requires that callers allow you the option to opt-out of receiving future automated calls. The opt-out feature should be announced during the automated menu when you answer a call and available for you to choose throughout the call.

Add Yourself to the National Do Not Call Registry

You can also add yourself to the National Do Not Call List by visiting DoNotCall.gov or calling 888-382-1222 from the phone you wish to register. If you register online, you must follow the link in the confirmation email that will be sent to you to complete the process.

By adding yourself to the list, you prohibit telemarketers from calling you, even if they are not using autodialers or prerecorded messages. Callers should cease all calls to you within thirty-one days.

If you have added yourself to the list but continue to receive sales calls after thirty-one days have passed, you can submit a complaint to the Federal Trade Commission.

Please note: The Do Not Call List specifically prohibits sales calls. You may still receive other types of calls, such as from political or charitable entities. It also does NOT stop debt collectors from calling you to collect on a debt.

If the TCPA guidelines are violated, you can sue for up to $500 for each violation (each robocall). You may also seek an injunction or both injunction and the money. If the violation of TCPA guidelines is willful, consumers can sue for damages up to three times, or $1,500 per violation.

FREQUENTLY ASKED QUESTIONS ABOUT DEBT COLLECTIONS

Can creditors come to your door?

People worry about a collector knocking on their door. Can a collector come to your door? No! In a debt collection scenario, only a sheriff, marshal, or private process server can come to your door, and that will happen *only* if you have been sued. They would be coming to your door to serve you with legal papers. That does not happen overnight, so any hint that a creditor or debt collector gives that they are going to show up at your house today or tomorrow is not true and is illegal. The only time it will happen is *after* a lawsuit is filed, and it will not be the debt collector who comes.

Can a debt collector threaten to sue me?

If a collection agency is threatening a person with a lawsuit, and they are not a law firm, their threat is meaningless and illegal because they cannot follow through on that threat. Be careful, however. As I pointed out earlier, these cases can be very technical. The debt collector may say, "If we cannot resolve this matter without litigation, the case may be turned over to a lawyer." That statement might be legal. I say "might" because if the collection agency regularly turns cases over to a law firm for litigation, then the statement is legal. However, if the agency does not turn cases over to a lawyer, it is a meaningless and deceptive threat and illegal. Again, one word or phrase can make a legal call illegal.

Can a debt collector talk to friends, relatives, or neighbors about my debt?

As you recall from a few pages ago, a debt collector *cannot* disclose the existence of your debt to a third party, that is, anyone other than you, your spouse, or your attorney. However, believe it or not, a debt collector can call anyone in an attempt to get what is known as "location information" or your new telephone number. Remember, your creditors and collection agencies know more about you than you can imagine—where you work, where you shop, etc.—and they use sophisticated software that helps them locate friends, relatives, and neighbors. It is perfectly legal for a debt collector to call anyone and ask if they know you or have your number.

Example: You changed your cell phone number, so the collection agency can't get a hold of you by phone. Your file gets sent to the investigative department, and investigators get to work trying to locate you. They call your neighbor and say, "Hi, I am just trying to find John Jones (you). Would you happen to have his address or telephone number?" The neighbor may know and may give them that information. Legal? Surprisingly, yes!

But what if during the call, the collector says, "He has an account with our agency that's in default, and it is important we reach him," and the neighbor gives him the number. Legal? No. Even though the collector did not mention that he was calling from a collection agency, the use of the word "default" by the debt collector indicated the existence of a delinquent debt to that third party.

What if the collector says, "I have an important business matter I need to speak with him about"? Legal? Yes. The collector was seeking your location information and did not disclose the existence of a debt.

What if the neighbor says, "I don't know," or "I am not going to give that information out"? If the collector hangs up and moves on, that is legal. But if a few days later, the collector calls back and again tries to get that information, the collector is harassing your neighbor, and that call becomes illegal.

A lawyer will help you understand your rights.

Can a collector call multiple times a day?

The short answer is yes, especially if the collector did not reach you on the previous calls.

But what if you are the sole caregiver for an elderly parent who lives with you and is being treated for a serious illness? Those collection calls constantly awaken the parent and agitate them, resulting in more work for the debtor, stress, and anxiety. Then the repeated calls become illegal.

Again, I don't want to encourage you to not pay your legitimate debts or to call a lawyer to help you "get out of paying a debt." What I want is for the system to be fair and balanced and for you to be educated and empowered to stand up for yourself.

Often, a violation of one statute is also a violation of another, and a lawyer can "stack" them.

What Are the Top Violations of the FDCPA?

The top violations are typically the following:

- Continued attempts to collect debt not owed (some are due to scams)
- Illegal or unethical communication tactics, including lying about the amount owed, improper notices, or disclosures
- Failure to validate or verify the debt after a request to do so—not providing proof that the debt is owed and that the debtor is the actual person who owes it
- Taking or threatening legal action
- False statements or false representation
- Improper contact or sharing of information from third-party disclosures
- Excessive phone calls

Except for the failure to include disclosures in a collection letter or failing to respond to a request for validation of the debt, most violations take place during telephone calls.

How do debt collection companies choose who to pursue? The ugly truth about data.

Every business on the planet wants to make money and be profitable. Even non-profits have to make enough money to cover costs. Every business uses its own system to maximize sales and profits, and today, every single one of those systems is driven by the data and the ease with which that data can be obtained through technology. By "data," I mean your personal information.

Many people today have those shopper's cards attached to their keychains for their favorite grocery store, gas station, or retailer. Consumers certainly appreciate the discounts they can receive when they use them, but do you know what they are really used for? You would rightly assume that it's a reward for shopping there. Some would understand that "it tells the retailer what we consumers are buying so the store knows what to make sure they have in stock." Both would be correct, but the truth is that every time you use a shopper card, debit card, or credit card, all your data—what you bought, when you bought it, how often you buy it, where you buy it, and where you search for it online—is being captured and stored by those companies.

Yes, they do use it to make sure their shelves are stocked, but the hidden truth is that the retailers then *sell your* information to companies you have never even heard of, who then resell it to other retailers. Those retailers, armed with your information, can target you with advertisements and special offers designed specifically to target you to get you to buy what they're selling, or start or continue using their cards.

My eyes were opened to this phenomenon many years ago. I was researching various stores online for a new light fixture. Within a day, I was receiving emails from stores, some of which I had been on their sites and some I had never heard of, with special deals on light fixtures. My data had been captured and passed along to other companies, who immediately reached out to me.

Do banks, lenders, and insurance companies gather and share information about you?

Banks and credit card companies have entire departments dedicated to deciding where each potential customer fits into their business model even before they loan you money. They already know what an "acceptable level of default" will be to them before they lend money. All of the data and other factors, including interest rates, default rates, lawsuits, lawsuit defense, are all part of their system.

That is part of the deck being stacked against you.

They also know that a large percentage of cases on which they file lawsuits, around 65%, are defaulted on. A default occurs when you fail to respond to a lawsuit filed against you by a lawyer working for a bank or collection agency. When you fail to respond by filing what is known as an Answer to the lawsuit, a court will accept as true what the lawyer alleged against you. The court finds you "liable" and enters a judgment against you. That judgment is then filed in the appropriate court and is placed as a lien against your home. The judgment sits there, earning interest, sometimes for years, until you decide to sell your home. Then, your realtor informs you that when you sell, before you get your money, the bank will get theirs, plus the interest. Again, the banks have this factored into their business model.

Just as banks and other original creditors have their business model figured out to the penny, debt buyers and collection agencies already know who will be sent off for litigation and who won't. Consumers with a high credit card balance, steady employment, who own their home or multiple homes, and are "locatable" (sometimes debtors move to other states and it takes a while to locate them) will be on the target list for a lawsuit.

If you don't own any assets or have a healthy savings or checking account, there is nothing for a bank to attach a judgment to, so they usually choose not to invest the money needed to even file a lawsuit. That said, a lawsuit is a very scary thing for most people. They don't know that a judgment against them is useless if they don't own a home or have other assets, so when they get sued, they will often find a way to get money—from a friend or relative—to make the case go away.

That sort of scare tactic does work, and creditors know this ahead of time. Remember, they have done their homework and already know what percentage of success they are likely to have before they start. It's a numbers game.

If You Win a Settlement, It May Still Count as Income

What? Yes! When a case is settled, a consumer receives a monetary settlement. Sometimes that monetary settlement is in the form of a check for $2,500, and sometimes it is having the credit card debt wiped clear as paid, settled in full, or both.

Creditors, for their tax benefit, want to write it off on their books as a loss or expense, so they send the consumer an IRS Form 1099 showing the payment, or if it included the removal of a debt, the value of that removal. Income is defined as *any* accession to wealth. If you no longer have to pay a $2,500 debt that you owed, you have grown your wealth in the amount of $5,000 (and you'll then be taxed on the $5,000).

If you settled your case for $3,000 and get a 1099 for that amount, that may not be accurate because part of that is attorney's fees or reimbursement for filing fees that the consumer paid, and thus, that entire portion is not income. That is definitely a topic you want to discuss with your accountant or tax professional because, as always, there are exceptions.

In the next chapter, we take a deep dive into one of the largest (and longest lasting) types of debt for millions of Americans—student loan debt.

WHAT YOU CAN DO RIGHT NOW

- Understanding how debt collection agencies work will give you an incredible advantage when settling your debt.
- Study the common violations of the Fair Debt Collection Practices Act (FDCPA) so you know when your rights have been violated and what is acceptable under the law. If you believe you have been violated, contact a consumer rights lawyer.
- Tired of the calls? Know the steps to take under the Telephone Consumer Protection Act (TCPA) to stop robocalls and add yourself to the National Do Not Call Registry.

ABOUT THE AUTHOR

Mark A. Carey, Esq.

Mark A. Carey is a New York and Georgia licensed attorney with over 30 years of litigation experience. Mark got his start as an Assistant District Attorney and those years of prosecuting criminals on behalf of victims of crime crystallized his desire to help those most vulnerable. Later, Mark would take those litigation skills to work as in-house counsel for two large collection agencies, and then as a managing attorney for a national collection firm. It was during those years that Mark witnessed first hand the inner workings and secrets the collection industry does not want consumers to know about. After leaving those positions, Mark began his own practice and continued his crusade to help consumers in need of guidance and legal help.

CHAPTER ELEVEN

FINANCIAL WELLNESS IS MORE ABOUT YOUR SELF-WORTH THAN NET WORTH

Understanding Your Relationship with Money
Hasnain Walji, Ph.D.

In earlier chapters we have covered some key concepts about money management and dealing with debt. Plus, we discussed a few things you can do to become more financially secure. In this chapter, we more closely examine your personal relationship with money to better understand how financial stress can affect your mental l health and what you can do about it.

Financial stress means different things to different people. For some, financial stress can be totally debilitating, while others only experience temporary bouts of stress and overcome it quickly.

Depending on what you're going through, you'll have different responses and emotions. For example, if you're experiencing financial stress, you may feel anxiety to find more money, shame, and worthlessness, or worries about your family's future; as well as physical symptoms like tension, headaches, trouble sleeping and even suicidal thoughts.

The good news is that increasing financial strength is less about the amount of money you do or don't have, and more about how well you manage your stress.

It is important that you give this chapter just as much attention as you have given previous chapters. Believe it or not, mastering stress management has the potential to make you just as much money (if not exponentially more) as any financial tip you could ever get from a top broker on Wall Street.

Each one of us has our own personal relationship with money. And, just like any intimate relationship, it can become toxic and unhealthy if we do not nurture it with care and maintain a delicate balance of harmony and discipline.

Maintaining your emotional health while fostering a low-stress environment is critical to effective money management, and ultimately, financial success. When stress levels run high, you can fall out-of-sync with yourself, which can be detrimental to your emotional health, and ultimately your bottom line.

Yes, financial security is a wonderful thing to have. Acquiring wealth and possessions is something many people aspire to achieve. However, the sense of security you seek will always elude you if live your life in a perpetual state of stress and ill health.

Learning how to master your emotional health is the greatest investment you can ever make. Self-worth will always be more valuable than net worth.

FINANCIAL STRESS CAN IMPACT YOUR MENTAL HEALTH.

Acquiring, managing, and maintaining financial success is not easy. If it were, every human on planet Earth would be wealthy (effectively rendering money worthless, of course). Many men and women have risen brilliantly to the top of the proverbial mountain, only to fall flat on their faces because they couldn't handle the pressure.

How would you describe your current emotional relationship with money? Few people ever slow down long enough to ask this question. Furthermore, few possess the wisdom to understand that this question should be asked in the first place.

Let's do a quick check in.

Can you think of a time recently when you had an emotional reaction to your financial situation? Maybe you felt so hopeless about your money situation that you shed actual tears?

Or it's possible that you stayed up at night and lost sleep over money, wondering how you were going to pay for everything. You might even find yourself thinking about money more often than you want to, either worrying about not having enough or planning on how you are going to spend it when you do have it.

You may have even lashed out and yelled at your loved ones, been negatively impacted at work, or felt extremely anxious or depressed because of money problems. Do you ever feel like no matter what you do, you are never fully satisfied with your financial state of affairs? Almost like you don't own your money, but it owns you.

You may not have ever given much thought to how finances affect your mental health until now. That's okay.

It is important to acknowledge that there is absolutely no reason to be feel ashamed or embarrassed for having strong feelings or reactions to finances. This is exactly what happens when stress becomes unmanageable.

And it is far more common than you think. Chances are that your friends and relatives have experienced the same type of stress and similar reactions when they have stood face-to-face with themselves and examined their own relationship with money. The statistics prove this out.

Here are a few stats that might put things into perspective:

- According to the APA's 2020 Stress in America Survey, about 64 percent of Americans report feeling stressed about money.[1]
- A recent survey by CompareCards.com by Lending Tree reported that crying about money is common with around 7 in 10 Americans saying they have cried over something related to their finances.[2]
- That same survey reports that money is a chief stressor for a significant portion of the population, with at least 4 in 10 Americans agreeing with the statement, "Nothing makes me cry more than money."[2]
- Thirty-one percent said that their overall debt situations made them emotional, and 20 percent said credit card debt in particular had made them cry.[2]
- A good portion consistently experienced a range of negative emotions such as anxiety, insecurity, and fear, and money emerged as the leading source of stress (44 percent).[3]

Remember, the next time you are crying into your pillow at night, wringing your hands, raging, or stressed to the max when you just don't feel like you can bare the weight of your financial stress: YOU ARE NOT ALONE.

Awareness is the key to change. Stepping out of the darkness of denial and into the light of truth is an important step toward realigning your emotional relationship with money. By acknowledging that you do have some loss of control when it comes to how you think and behave about money matters, you can regain control.

Let's go deeper.

MODERN MAN PROCESSES EMOTIONAL RESPONSES IN THE FORM OF A PHYSICAL REACTION

Believe it or not, the stress you feel and the emotional reactions you have about money matters are very primal.

Money makes it possible for you to have food, clothing, and shelter. It allows you transportation to get to and from work, so you can earn a livelihood, which provides for your family. Money makes sure your basic needs are met. Sure, the extras are a plus. It's fun to go on vacations, go out to eat at a nice restaurant or spoil yourself with something extravagant. But, the bottom line is, money provides your basic human needs.

When you don't have enough, or your sense of security is being threatened, it sets off a primal chain reaction.

For example, if a collector call comes in, or the prospect of an unexpected car repair expense looms, along come distressing physical symptoms such as a racing heart, raised blood pressure, sweaty palms, nauseated stomach and more. They come about when, for whatever reason, our mind tells us that we are under a threat. The body's systems respond immediately, flooding us with certain chemicals (such as adrenalin and cortisol), to prepare us to fight off the threat.

Popularly known as the *'Fight or Flight'* response, we have inherited this from our hunter-gatherer ancestors. Over the centuries, when hunter-gatherers were stalking for their next meal, they often came face-to-face with a very real threat – such as confronting a Sabre tooth tiger while hunting.

In an instant, they would have reacted. They had to make a choice and fast: either battle the tiger or run for their lives.

This helps to explain why we experience our strong emotional reactions to money matters. The heart and breathing rate escalate as the body tries to deliver abundant oxygen to the muscles in our arms and legs, ready to fight or flight.

In modern times, the debt collector is the Sabre tooth tiger! (They can be very aggressive and threatening, right!?) When we are in fear of losing our homes, or not being able to put food on the table, or losing something we have worked hard for, or not getting something, we want, out comes caveman (or woman).

Nowadays, it would be highly unlikely for us to be attacked by a wild animal (although it does happen). Yet, even in the modern world, there are many perceived threats (whether real or imagined) we face each day that affect us emotionally, such as relationship difficulties, financial worries, or even sitting in traffic jams. The mind does not differentiate what type of threat we are under – it just signals a threat, and the body acts accordingly.

Unlike our ancestors, we never actually resolve the situation. In ancient times, they would have faced the tiger and fought or run. This would have burned off those powerful anxious chemicals, allowing the balance to be restored to the brain after the threat passed. In other words, the tiger (threat) caused stress, stress stimulated chemical release, fight or flight encouraged physical activity, physical activity burned chemicals, and the body returned to normal once the threat is over.

Today our threats often go unresolved. The chemicals kick in, but they have nowhere to go. So, they fester and continue to affect us long after the event has resolved itself. This can cause ongoing anxiety and stress.

Furthermore, our perceived threats are often internal issues, rather than actual external dangers. They are more likely to be our own mindset, thoughts, and challenges. We can't fight or run away from them, but we still experience the rapid heart rate, shallow breathing and sweating, the butterflies, and an inability to sleep.

THE LINK BETWEEN EMOTIONAL WEALTH AND FINANCIAL HEALTH

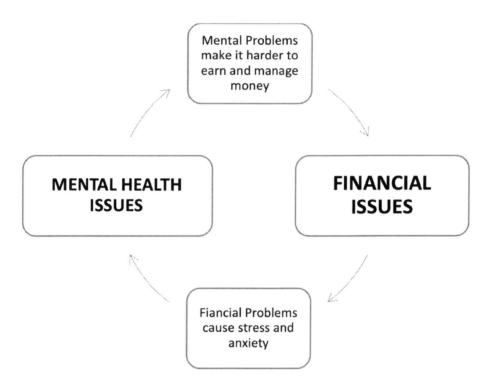

Mental health and money problems are often intricately linked. What we think about affects how we feel emotionally. What happens to us generally affects what we think about. Thus, there is an intrinsic link between our emotional and mental health. For some of us, finances are often the center of our universe. When we place this much value on financial status, our relationship with money greatly impacts the relationship we have with ourselves.

We measure our self-worth by our net worth. When the chips are up, we celebrate and consider that we are good, responsible, contributing members of society. When the pendulum swings in the other direction, we shame ourselves and beat ourselves up, blaming ourselves for being so worthless and useless.

This type of instability can be too much to bear. This is why so many people get depressed and even become suicidal because of financial stress and their unhealthy relationship with money. In fact, research shows money stress can make people up to 20 times more likely to make a suicide attempt.[6]

Covid-19 pandemic has added to the challenges. Household budgets have been put under pressure with joblessness along with rising prices. The adjustments of everyday life have taken a toll on the mental wellbeing of the nation. During the Covid crisis, people with mental health problems faced a much higher risk of financial hardship compared to the wider population. In the August 2021 edition of the *Verywell Mind Mental Health Tracker*, researchers report that Americans are feeling less affected by COVID-19 compared to financial problems. 27% of these surveyed placed financial problems as their *"biggest source of stress over the past 30 days'* as compared to 16% opting for Covid-19 as the biggest stressor.[7]

If we are not healthy mentally, it can set off a perpetual stress cycle that results in ill health, which ultimately leads to poor financial decisions and money mismanagement.

We neglect self-care when our daily responsibilities become too overwhelming, which means we neglect our finances. This leads to further stress and anxiety, which leads to even worse decisions.

We live in a constant "caveman" state—minus the tiger. Soon, this becomes a spiral downward. This is how people go bankrupt, get foreclosed upon, lose their businesses, and sadly hit bottom. And, truth be told, much of it could have been avoided with stress management and a healthy relationship with finances.

It is widely known that financial problems can have an adverse effect upon on mental health. Not having enough money can be highly stressful, leading to everything from migraines to feelings of hopelessness and depression.[4] People with money problems have higher rates of anxiety and insomnia, which can greatly impair your ability to think clearly.

Experts believe that financial insecurity is linked not just to stress and anxiety but can also cause relationship problems between spouses and impaired job performance.[5]

We're more likely to make poor health choices when trying to deal with stress. To discuss this further, let's put into perspective how financial stress negatively impacts mental and emotional health.

According to the American Psychological Association[5], among those experiencing financial stress:

- 42 percent report sleep problems such as lying awake, unable to sleep
- 36 percent report overeating or eating unhealthy foods
- 27 percent report skipping meals.
- 13 percent report drinking alcohol to manage stress

In no uncertain terms, you must have emotional wealth to sustain financial health. What does this mean?

This means that you make your health a priority ABOVE ALL ELSE. You must be rich in your physical, emotional, mental, and spiritual health in order to have a fulfilling relationship with money.

You make sure you eat right (we'll get to this) and get plenty of restful sleep every night. You take it easy on the alcohol. No drugs. You keep your stress level low by refusing to participate in the unnecessary dramas of life. You participate in activities you enjoy. You make loved ones your priority. You learn to say "no" to avoid overloading an already packed schedule.

Conversely, it means you remain steadfast and committed to getting your finances in order and keeping them in order. Financial security and emotional health are interdependent. You will feel a lot less stressed if you follow the principles outlined in this book consistently.

In simple terms, you continually monitor your emotional and financial health and adjust swiftly when you feel out of balance. Absolutely nothing is worth your peace of mind. What good is financial security if you aren't around to enjoy it with your family? Is it even possible to be stress-free when you are up to your eyeballs in debt and one step away from being homeless?

You are truly wealthy when you have your health and your finances in order, when you maintain that delicate balance mentioned earlier. Of course, your health comes first. The money is a just a bonus. Adopt this mentality and you are sure to capture financial freedom and true success.

NUTRITIONAL CONSIDERATIONS TO MINIMIZE THE EFFECTS OF FINANCIAL STRESS

As a nutritionist, I simply must mention the valuable role food plays in our lives, especially as it relates to emotional balance and stress reduction. Stress and eating habits have a significant connection. When it comes to food and stress, one of the best things you can do for your body is to choose a healthy, balanced diet.

This is because during the fight or flight response your body has an immediate and direct impact on digestion. It slows the contractions of the digestive muscles and reduces enzymes and other substances needed for digestion. Hence, when you're under stress, making changes to your eating style could be the key to feeling better.

HOW FOOD AFFECTS MOOD

The connection between nutrition and emotions arises from the intimate relationship between your brain and your gut, sometimes called the "second brain." Your gut is home to billions of bacteria that influence the production of certain chemical substances (Dopamine and Serotonin) that constantly carry messages from the gut to the brain.

A wholesome diet promotes the growth of "good" bacteria, which in turn positively affects production of Dopamine and Serotonin amongst other neurotransmitters. An unhealthy diet on the other hand, fosters inflammation that hinders the production of these chemical substances. A healthy dose results in positive messages which are then reflected in your emotions.

For example, sugar, is considered a major contributor of inflammation and feeds "bad" bacteria in the gut. Despite causing a temporary spike in "feel good" neurotransmitters, it is followed by a crash resulting a bad mood. Experts tell us that healthy diets can help with symptoms of depression and anxiety and unhealthy diets have been linked to an increased risk of dementia or stroke.

FOODS THAT HELP YOU BE HEALTHY

Here's a quick overview of what to look for next time you're in the grocery store.

Studies have shown that preservatives, food colorings and other additives may cause or worsen hyperactivity and depression. So, look for foods minimally processed and always include fresh fruits and vegetables. Antioxidants are effective inflammation fighters are especially plentiful in green leafy vegetables.

Fermented foods, (such as sauerkraut, kimchi, miso, tempeh and the fermented kombucha) are packed with probiotics, which help in maintain a good balance of the good bacteria on your digestive tract.

FOODS TO AVOID

- Foods high in fat and sugar – these will provide a short burst of energy and short-term relief, but this will be quickly followed by a 'low' period when your blood sugar levels crash, making you feel worse in the long-term.

  We live in a society that promotes high-sugar drinks and food. Be mindful about what you are putting into your body. It might be an adjustment to cut the sugar, but before long, you will notice a positive difference and experience a mood boost.

- Alcohol – turning to alcohol to deal with stress may have a momentary calming effect on the body. However, in the long-term it takes a toll on overall health and well-being.

  Alcohol is linked to sleep problems, depression and anxiety – all things manifested by financial stress. Alcohol will only make you feel worse, and it will only make your problems worse. You need clarity to make difficult financial decisions. Steer clear of the alcohol.

FOODS & NUTRIENTS TO INCLUDE

- Fruits and vegetables: Eating a diet rich in fresh fruit and vegetables will ensure you get the nutrients you need to stay powered up to face your financial situation head on. When your body is feeling stressed, it needs to use more nutrients than it normally would. Aim to eat at least five portions of fruit and vegetables every day, especially foods containing vitamins B, C and magnesium.

- B vitamins provide the body with energy after a period of stress. Folate, a type of B vitamin helps with dopamine production. They are found in bananas, leafy greens, nuts, seeds, meat, fish, and dairy products.
- Vitamin C. The adrenal glands responsible for the production of stress hormones require copious amounts of Vitamin C. Vitamin C rich foods are oranges, tomatoes, peppers, leafy greens and broccoli.
- Magnesium is known to help to relax muscles and reduce anxiety. A magnesium deficiency can hurt the bacteria in your gut and cause depression and anxiety-like symptoms. Nuts, beans, lentils, whole grains and leafy greens are all high in magnesium.
- Vitamin D helps with the production of serotonin. Though we usually get it from exposure to sunlight, if you are deficient in vitamin D, taking a supplement is advised

In addition to a healthy diet, the following vitamins and herbal supplements can be helpful in stress management.
- **Vitamin B complex:** known for improving cognitive performance.
- **Magnesium** for muscle and nerve function, and it helps you relax,
- **Valerian Root** to help with nervousness, anxiety, and sleep disturbances and therefore supplementing with valerian root can help reduce stress.

TIPS FOR EFFECTIVELY NAVIGATING FINANCIAL STRESS

We've talked a lot about financial stress, emotional health, and your personal relationship with money.

Here are 12 recommendations to help you forge ahead on your journey towards financial freedom and security:

1. **The first step is to understand what you can control and what you cannot.** Some things are simply out of your control. Recognize what these things are early in the game and let them go. Dwelling on things you can't control wastes precious energy you could be using to tackle problems with real-world solutions. Worrying about things beyond your control is sure to cause even more stress and frustration,

which is an unnecessary waste of precious energy. Instead, focus on the things you can change in the short term – however small they may seem. A small savings in your food spending, for example, will give you a sense of accomplishment and reduce your stress levels.

2. As recommended elsewhere in this book, **assess where you are.** List what you have and what you owe. What debts do you have, and what are the interest rates on each? Evaluate where and how your money is coming in and going out. What are your expenses, what do you typically spend money on, and what's left over? Track your spending. Research shows that tracking can be an effective tool. Remember, awareness leads to change.

3. **Don't try to make financial decisions all at once.** When faced with rising bills and not enough income to cover them, it's easy to get overwhelmed. Spread your financial decisions out over time and tackle them one at a time. As the saying goes, Rome wasn't built in a day. You didn't get here overnight, and you won't get out overnight. And that is okay. Remember, slow and steady wins the race.

4. **Talk to friends and family.** It's uncomfortable talking about money with those close to us. However, sharing your financial stress with a trusted friend or family member helps in figuring out how to move forward. Often, speaking about your financial issues will help you put them into perspective and help you figure out what to do next. Remember, MOST people have struggled or even cried about their own financial stress. You are not alone.

5. **Make a plan and stick to it. The chapters in this book are designed to help you** take stock of your financial situation and identify where money causes you stress. Once you have **identified your financial stressors, make a plan,** commit to it, and review it regularly. Writing a plan and sticking to it can reduce stress. Otherwise, things will feel random and uncertain. Uncertainly leads to anxiety.

6. **Be mindful of how you deal with stress.** Faced with financial issues, especially during tough economic times, some people tend to turn to unhealthy activities such as smoking, drinking, drug addiction, gambling, or emotional eating. If these behaviors are causing you distress, consider seeking help from a mental health professional

before the problem gets worse. Remember, your emotional health ALWAYS comes first.

7. **Stay away from temptation.** Limit your time shopping (whether at the mall or online) and consider alternative social activities. Leave your credit cards at home and just carry the amount of cash you can afford to spend.

8. **Ask for support.** Surround yourself with people you trust who will support your financial goals and want to help you reach them.

9. **Make time for relationships.** When under financial stress, you may feel the urge to avoid socializing and isolate. Yet this is a critical time to reach out to the people who mean the most to you. This is a time to build a much-needed support system that can help you cope with stress, improve your relationship with money, and increase your self-worth.

10. **Don't indulge in negative self-talk.** Try to look at stressful situations in a positive light. Replace negative thoughts, such as "Nothing going as planned," with thoughts, such as "OK, things went differently than planned. But I can handle it." Seek help from someone who can help you cope and teach you helpful techniques for reducing negative thoughts.

11. **Stay active.** Physical activity can improve your mood if you're feeling low. No, you don't need an expensive gym membership. Go for a walk - never underestimate the power of a stroll in the park. Research shows that a 90-minute walk can reduce activity in the brain linked to repetitive negative thoughts. Exercise regulates the fight/flight response because that is what the body is designed to do when it perceives a threat.

12. **Mindfulness exercises.** A simple yet effective form of relaxation is to slow your breathing down to diaphragmatic breathing. If you slow your breathing down it will also slow down your heart rate and in turn allow the blood flow to return to where it should be. Meditating for 15 minutes three or four times weekly can help reduce your cortisol levels. Also, practicing yoga calms your nervous system to reduce inflammation.

Remember - next time you notice your stress levels are so high that you are no longer being productive, or your anxiety is making you miserable and sick, take a step back. Trying harder has the potential to make things worse. Take a breath, center yourself and refer to one of the strategies to get yourself back on track.

Work to maintain a healthy relationship with your finances. Always put your emotional health first. Stay the course and before you know it, you will achieve the positive financial position you are striving for. And, when you get there – you will be able to enjoy it and sustain it.

[1] https://www.apa.org/news/press/releases/stress/2020/report-october

[2] https://www.prnewswire.com/news-releases/comparecards-survey-finds-nearly-7-in-10-americans-have-cried-about-money-300943154.html

[3] https://theharrispoll.com/new-research-shows-money-is-the-leading-source-of-happiness-and-stress/

[4] www.everydayhealth.com/news/how-avoid-health-risks-come-with-financial-stress

[5] www.apa.org/news/press/releases/stress/2012/report-summary.aspx

[6] https://www.health.com/money/financial-stress-suicide-risk

[7] https://www.verywellmind.com/mental-health-tracker-financial-stress-5197905

ABOUT THE AUTHOR

Hasnain Walji, Ph.D.

Hasnain Walji is a researcher, educator and writer who has authored 26 books on nutrition and natural medicine. He has a keen interest in connecting the dots between technology and human behavior. As a thought leader, the hallmark of his leadership is to think outside the box so that the businesses and non-profit organizations he is engaged with will remain relevant and progressive as they confront new realities and challenges.

In the past, Hasnain's research has focused on integrative health care and behavioral finance. More recently, his efforts have been more concentrated on persuasive technology designed to change users' attitudes and behaviors through encouragement and social influence.

Currently, Hasnain serves as Vice President of Knowledge Management at the MBT Group. He is also the is lead content author of the Financial Strength Builder™ Program – an acclaimed financial literacy training tool used to help build financial strength in the American household. The program helps people resolve financial challenges and create plans that provide for increased savings, reduced debt and wiser daily spending choices.

CHAPTER TWELVE

SOLVING YOUR STUDENT DEBT PROBLEMS

with Larry R. Taylor, Ph.D.

As every person's financial needs and capabilities are different, the advice given here may or may not apply to your specific situation. Sound student loan management should be a part of your overall financial picture. For optimal results, consult a qualified planner or tax professional before making changes to your student loan debt.

Many Americans have long held the belief that the key to a great job, homeownership, and a financially secure future must include a college education. As a result, tens of thousands start this journey each year, with little thought about how the debt will be repaid, its future impact on their budget, or the potential return on investment. This has been a pattern for well over two decades. It's no wonder student loan debt has become a serious financial problem for such a substantial segment of the US population.

Over forty-five million individuals have some type of student loan debt. In fact, in 2020, 54% of college attendees took on debt, including student loans, to pay for their education at an average of $37,584 of student loan debt per borrower.[3] Barely a year later, according to the US Student Loan Debt Statistics for 2021, the total student loan debt exceeds $1.71 trillion.[4] It's safe to say that student loan debt is a pervasive problem in the United

---

3 Daniel Kurt, "Student Loan Debt: 2020 Statistics and Outlook," updated October 25, 2021, *Investopedia*, https://www.investopedia.com/student-loan-debt-2019-statistics-and-outlook-4772007.

4 "A Look at the Shocking Student Loan Debt Statistics for 2021," updated Jan. 27, 2021, Student Loan Hero, https://studentloanhero.com/student-loan-debt-statistics.

States, affecting borrowers and frequently their families. The trend will likely continue.

Student loan debt has many facets that are grounded in the fiscal and psychological worlds. Most everyone tends to focus on the numbers. The size of the debt, how to help borrowers, making changes to the programs, and more. It is possibly the largest debt many borrowers will have, perhaps aside from their mortgage.

But not enough attention is given to the psychological dimensions affecting borrowers and families. Dealing with such an oppressive problem that prevents future goal accomplishments can make many feel that there's no end in sight. They will have the debt until they die, with no hope of paying it off or accomplishing any of their goals. Also, the daily stress and anxiety of worrying about how to solve the problem can take a toll on physical and mental health. Compounding the mental anguish is the complexity of repayment programs and the process of resolving problems within the bureaucracy of loan servicers. Your solution, regardless of your situation, will require personal commitment and continued focus.

What we intend to accomplish in this chapter is to offer a foundation for making positive improvements about how you manage and solve problems with your student loan debt. We also would like you to buy into the idea that your student loan debt must be treated as a part of your overall financial strategy. It's not an isolated debt as, for many people, it's the largest one aside from a mortgage (and in some cases more!).

In the following sections we will cover:

- The psychology of student loan debt and how to reframe it to create a success path that matches your specific objectives.
- How to assess your potential for solving student loan problem.
- How to deal with serious problems from payment challenges to serious delinquency.
- Why taking no action can be far more severe than with conventional unsecured debt such as credit cards.
- If you should consider a financial "partner" to help with your student loan repayment strategy.
- How to choose the best professional to help with student loan advice and problem-solving.

- Why taking multiple "views" of your student loan finances is a critical success factor (interest, motivation, commitment).
- Imminent changes in student loan programs you should be aware of in an income-driven repayment plan.

By the end of this chapter, you should have greater clarity as to your next steps. Through the additional knowledge gained here, we hope you'll have more peace of mind about your situation. If you're facing serious challenges, please take action and use the information found here to the best of your abilities. If you are not facing challenges, you still need to regularly evaluate your loans, costs, and repayment strategy. The right strategy will balance your ability to repay debt and accomplish other financial goals such as investing, planning for retirement, family, and business matters.

THE EASIEST MONEY

Getting money for college is one of the easiest things you'll ever do. It's as simple as filling out paperwork and signing the loan documents. One of the challenges is that, unlike a mortgage, you're getting multiple loans throughout your education. Each time, you must reapply and sign new documents. So, what starts as a $10,000 loan for year one, can turn into $40,000 or more if you complete your degree in four years. And if you're interested in taking more time to complete your degree, add more debt to that. Don't take that for granted, as it will have to be repaid.

Easy money is easy to spend and even easier to lose track of until the day you start to repay it several years down the road. Commit to finishing your education as quickly as possible and get on with earning a great paycheck while comfortably repaying the student debt. Of course, if you already have the debt, it's time to make the commitment to a solution that works for you while not hindering the other goals. It is absolutely possible!

YOU ARE NOT ALONE—WHO HAS STUDENT LOAN DEBT?

Graduate students make up only 14% of college enrollment. However, they account for 40% of the student debt issued. PhDs make up the largest share of degree-seeking students at 23%. And the median debt loads for professionals range from $42,000 for MBAs and $161,722 for medical students.[5]

In 2019, Experian reported the following breakdown of student debt by age:[6]

AGE	TOTAL DEBT	AVERAGE CREDIT SCORE
24 and younger	$123B	674
25 to 34	$454.6B	665
35 to 49	$406.8B	682
50 to 61	$171.3B	709
62 and older	$42.8B	750

Borrowers between the ages of thirty-five and forty-nine had the highest delinquency rates, meaning the age group was more likely to stop paying their student loans. A total of $15.5 billion in federal student loans held by borrowers in this category were delinquent between thirty and ninety days. Despite these delinquency rates, Experian data shows that most of those consumers managed to pay enough on their debt to maintain a reasonable credit score of around 682 and to stay out of delinquency.

---

5 "The CSLP Financial Advisor Program," CSLA Institute, January 14, 2021, https://cslainstitute.org/the-cslp-program-content/.

6 Stefan Lembo Stolba, "Student Loan Debt Reaches Record High as Most Repayment Is Paused," Experian, February 24, 2021, https://www.experian.com/blogs/ask-experian/state-of-student-loan-debt/.

SECTION I

UNDERSTANDING YOUR STUDENT DEBT

This section is about getting a clear understanding of your debt and the programs available for repayment. By the end, you'll be better informed to make decisions about choices that are in your best interest.

STUDENT LOAN DEBT IS MORE COMPLEX THAN YOU MIGHT THINK

Despite what many financial experts and consumers believe, student loans and the decisions to be made about them can be complex. Student loans are different from your credit card or mortgage debt. There are many programs to repay. It's not necessary to get into the details of all of these but, to make a point, they are: Pay As You Earn (PAYE), Income-Based Repayment (IBR), New IBR, Old IBR, Income-Contingent Repayment (ICR), Graduated Repayment, Extended Repayment, and Revised Pay As You Earn (REPAYE). Yes, it's complicated. But in this chapter, we'll help you find out what you have and how to leverage resources to make the best decisions to solve your problem and get on the right path.

The first step is to understand the primary loan types and identify the details of all of your loans.

FEDERAL STUDENT LOANS

First, the federal government provides many flavors of loan types, which should not be a surprise. While the intent was to make it easier for people to repay, over the years, it's become more complicated. As we will restate multiple times, because of the complexity of repayment options and your individual circumstances, getting an expert's help is recommended.

Federally backed loans are relatively easy. Credit isn't a factor unless you are delinquent with other student loans. These loans are fixed-rate loans that can be repaid over ten, twenty, or thirty years depending on the program you choose. Every year, the government sets the federal loan rate. This means you may have some loans at one rate and others at a different rate. This is where the discussion about consolidation comes into play. For example, when you started school, your first-year loan may have been at 4%, Next year, you take out a loan for the next tuition, and this loan is at 5%, etc. Again, your rate on any given loan is fixed, but you will have multiple loans at different rates. A consolidation bundles all the loans into one at the average of all the rates you had.

There are other implications of consolidations, so please review with a financial professional to see if this is ultimately in your best interest.

Federal Loan Protections

Another standout feature of federal loans is that you have several protections available should you run into financial trouble. This is called forbearance. It can be used should you lose your job and have a medical issue, or your income drops substantially. It's one of the best parts of federal loans. While in forbearance, you aren't required to make loan payments. You must apply for forbearance and identify the reason, but it's not difficult to obtain.

PRIVATE STUDENT LOANS

Private student loans are not offered by the federal government. They are provided by credit card companies and a host of other firms. These loans are more traditional in the sense that they are a personal loan or like credit card debt. They generally require good credit and possibly a cosigner. Private loans generally do not have such great benefits as federal loans in the case of financial problems. If you have a financial issue, you'll need to negotiate with the creditor, which may or may not work out to your liking. You may also incur additional fees and interest. You will definitely have more interaction with the creditor, and should financial problems happen, it may be more difficult to get the help you need.

Private Student Loan Risks

Private student loans are offered through third parties, such as credit card companies, banks, and other organizations like online personal finance companies. They usually require above-average credit, sufficient income, and possibly a cosigner.

Today's basic TV pitch is that you'll get a lower interest rate, but that's not always true. Sometimes their rates may be substantially higher than your existing federal loans. Suppose you've taken an inventory of your loans. In that case, you might find that your federal loans have reasonably low rates, often less than 5%, but it varies based on your loan dates.

Private loan financing companies often propose consolidating all your loans to have a single payment with a merged interest rate (the average interest rate of all your federal loans). That may sound good, but does it truly save you money? Get an independent analysis of the numbers if you aren't comfortable in calculating them.

As we've stated, private loans differ in one major way from federal loans as they lack provisions for financial hardship. Working with private loan creditors may be more difficult, requiring more time and explanations than with federal loans.

Private lenders have a wide range of terms. Often, private loans are more difficult to obtain based on tighter restrictions. Still, they can be discharged in bankruptcy or can be settled for less than what is owed.

A thorough analysis is recommended before making that jump to a private refinance because once you leave the protection of federal loans, there's no going back.

THE CONSOLIDATION MILLS AND REFINANCING

One approach that is very popular today is student loan consolidation and refinancing. Literally hundreds of companies are pitching this as a solution to improve your finances. Unfortunately, many of these companies are call centers with sales staff who have little to no experience in personal finance. Before using a company pitching student loan "solutions and consolidations," review our top ten list of questions on page 149 to ask before choosing someone to help with your student loan questions.

Having said that, Direct Consolidations are completely legitimate processes and can have immense value if done correctly for the right conditions. And keep in mind, you can complete the process online, and at no cost. If you are unsure about any part of the process, contact a student loan advisor to determine if it is in your best interest to consolidate at this time.

Here is the direct link to the instructions:

https://studentaid.gov/app-static/images/Instructions.pdf

Refinancing your student debt is another matter. Many companies are offering rates that may be very attractive and ultimately it may make sense. It's up to you and your financial advisor to decide. Finally, as we note throughout this chapter, moving from Federal loans to private financing does eliminate the government protections such as deferment.

To recap, keep these caveats in mind:

Caveat #1: Many companies suggest that you can save money by consolidating your loans and lowering your interest rate so that you're essentially getting the benefit of the average interest rate of all of your loans versus having one loan at 2%, for example, and another loan at 7%. It sounds great on the surface but could be financially deadly. Consolidations need to occur at the right time for your specific situation and financial goals. Done at the wrong time, they could jeopardize your potential loan forgiveness if that is something you are planning on. For more information, meet with a qualified financial advisor with advanced knowledge of student loans and consolidations as every situation is different.

Caveat #2: Private loan refinancing. Almost hourly, advertisements on television and radio tell you how their lives were saved because they refinanced with company XYZ. While you might land a better rate, be sure to understand what you are losing. Federal loan protections can help you if you become seriously ill or lose your job. If you have a private loan, you could be placed into collections after missing several months of payments. You have to judge your personal situation and determine which is most important.

It's possible that private loan financing is a good option for you, but as we mentioned earlier, you must generally have good credit and the income to qualify. Often, when people respond to those ads, they discover that their current financial situation may not be strong enough for approval.

THE PANDEMIC PAUSE

Since March 2020, due to the COVID-19 pandemic, there has been a pause in the requirement to make federal student loan debt payments. The CARES Act also paused interest accrual and any debt collection activity.[3] If you continued to make payments, you could request a refund for payments made from March 2020 until the resumption date, which is scheduled for February 1, 2022.

You should monitor your email (and spam), texts, and postal mail to notify you when your next payment is due, which will be sometime around February 1, 2022. You can also log into StudentAid.gov to find out your loan servicer as, for many, this will be automatically assigned. FedLoan Servicing (MyFedLoan.org) will no longer service loans.

New PSLF Changes

Additionally, the Department of Education (DOE) has announced numerous other changes that apply to those in Public Service Loan Forgiveness (PSLF) programs.

- A limited PSLF waiver will now allow all payments by student borrowers to count toward PSLF, regardless of loan program or payment plan.[4]

Many of the previous problems that occurred with borrowers who applied for forgiveness should be solved by this action. Borrowers were often denied because they were in the wrong loan program to receive forgiveness. This waiver will allow student borrowers to count all payments made on loans from the Federal Family Education Loan (FFEL) Program or Perkins Loan Program. It will also waive restrictions on the type of repayment plan and the requirement that payments be made in the full amount and on time for all borrowers.

---

3 "COVID-19 Emergency Relief and Federal Student Aid," Federal Student Aid, https://studentaid.gov/announcements-events/covid-19.

4 "U.S. Department of Education Announces Transformational Changes to the Public Service Loan Forgiveness Program, Will Put Over 550,000 Public Service Workers Closer to Loan Forgiveness" (U.S. Department of Education, October 6, 2021), https://www.ed.gov/news/press-releases/us-department-education-announces-transformational-changes-public-service-loan-forgiveness-program-will-put-over-550000-public-service-workers-closer-loan-forgiveness.

To receive these benefits and count any additional payments made but previously denied, borrowers will have to submit a PSLF form[5] by October 31, 2022. This is a single application used to certify employment and evaluate a borrower for forgiveness.

Additional changes to the PSLF program include:

- Borrowers who currently have FFEL, Perkins, or other Non-Direct Loans, will receive benefit of this limited waiver if they apply to consolidate into the Direct Loan Program and submit a PSLF form by October 31, 2022. The waiver applies to loans taken out by students.

- Credit will automatically be provided to PSLF for military service members and federal employees using federal data matches. The DOE will implement data matches next year (2022) to give these borrowers credit toward PSLF without an application. This solves a problem for service members who have paused payments while on active duty but were not getting credit toward PSLF.

- Denied PSLF applications will be reviewed for errors and give borrowers the ability to have their PSLF determinations reconsidered. These actions will help identify and address servicing errors or other issues that have prevented borrowers from getting the PSLF credit they deserve.

For more information, visit this site: StudentAid.gov/PSLFWaiver.

Now is the perfect time to act, evaluate student loans, and consult with a professional who can help determine your best course of action and answer questions.

ASSESSING YOUR NUMBERS AND COLLECTING YOUR LOAN DATA

What is your financial budget? Don't know? It's time you find out. Your best solutions and strategies will come when you have all the data. That means knowing your complete income and expense picture. Identify other near-term bonuses or cash infusions. Do you have other sources for additional income, such as a side hustle?

---

[5] "Public Service Loan Forgiveness (PSLF) & Temporary Expanded PSLF Form," Federal Student Aid (Department of Education), https://studentaid.gov/sites/default/files/public-service-application-for-forgiveness.pdf.

As for expenses, more than likely, on the first pass of creating your budget, you will miss certain expenditures. It has been our experience that we all tend to spend more than we realize, given the convenience of debit and credit cards. We may also forget about the automatic subscriptions. Take a month and document every expense every day. You'll have a more accurate picture of your outflow.

The best approach is to review your bank and credit card statements to create a detailed monthly cash flow to understand the resources you have to apply to the problem. Having that data clear in your mind and on paper is essential for when you speak with the loan servicer about resolving past due payments. It will also be helpful when you speak to a financial planner to evaluate the best student loan repayment plan for you at this time.

IN TROUBLE: WHAT TO PAY FIRST?

Student loans should be at the top of your list in the hierarchy of debts to pay, right there with the IRS. You do have some leeway but getting too far behind can be trouble. The government can seize money when you least expect it, leaving virtually nothing except the cash on hand. Garnishments can be placed on wages and other assets, liens on property and bank accounts. You could lose tax refunds and any licenses suspended. Of course, you must prioritize basic living expenses. Still, it's equally vital that you stay in contact with your lenders and, if applicable, the IRS. Avoidance is not a solution and will make your problems far worse.

BANKRUPTCY AND SETTLEMENT OF STUDENT DEBT

Student debt is rarely dischargeable in bankruptcy and can be a difficult process to negotiate. Generally, you would have to prove insolvency to eliminate federal student debt. To determine if that is possible, you should seek the services of an attorney who thoroughly understands student loan law, ideally working in concert with a certified financial advisor.

The range of relief available for those with federal loans should help alleviate some of the financial pressure by delaying required student loan payments. After you have reestablished your financial footing, you must file a change in status to resume payments and end forbearance. If you are on an income-based repayment plan, changes in income can be reflected and potentially reduce the requirement payment. Keep in mind that your financial professional can help determine the most appropriate repayment plan based on your situation.

In case you're wondering, you can't settle federal student loan debt for pennies on the dollar like you may be able to with other debt. If someone has $300,000 in student loan debt, they must eventually pay or meet qualifying requirements for loan forgiveness. It's also important to know that when any type of debt is forgiven, the IRS may consider this as taxable income. They will send you a Form 1099 in the amount of the forgiven debt. That will trigger higher taxes and another potential problem. Imagine that you go from a $50,000 tax bracket to $300,000 and receive a bill for $30,000 or more in new taxes! That is another reason to consider having a well-informed financial professional in your court so you understand the risks and rewards for the choices you make. If you are in a public service loan forgiveness program, you won't incur tax on the forgiven amount.

SECTION II

THE PSYCHOLOGY BEHIND YOUR STUDENT DEBT

It's important to understand that if you have student debt problems, you're not alone. There are numerous resources available to help with both the financial problems and the difficult emotions surrounding how to cope.

FACING THE PROBLEM

In some cases, debt problems can be challenging to face. Many people just can't bear to look at the numbers. Some of my certified public accountant (CPA) and certified financial planner (CFP) friends have had clients break down in their office when looking at student debt. (If this is you, be sure to check out the section "So, Where Do I Find Professional Help?" on page 146 to find out more about how they can help you, too.

Face your problem and fears, and then align yourself with solutions. Fear and anxiety are often about worry over the unknown and being out of control. Tackling your problem with the help of others is a great way to alleviate those negative feelings and stress.

YOUR NUMBERS AND MINDSET

Regardless of the level of your student loan debt, it is critically important that you thoroughly assess your situation and know your capabilities and limitations. Here's how to take a temperature check:

- Verify the loans you have and the specific details, such as interest rate, the amount owed, and the type of loan.
- What is the payment?
- Does the payment change during the life of the loan?
- What is your interest rate?
- What are the fees if you are late or miss a payment?
- What are the processes if you run into a financial challenge?

It pays to know those answers. I'd recommend you do this assessment at least yearly and document the date you did it.

The next part of the assessment involves determining the effect the payment may have on your monthly budget. Keeping in mind that these payments can go on for potentially dozens of years into the future, how is it affecting decisions surrounding you or your family's specific goals?

- For this one, look for some indication of how your student loans affect your levels of stress, anxiety, and worry.
- Are you struggling to make payments?
- Do you frequently make late payments?
- Are you presently behind with payments?
- If you are behind, how many have you missed?
- Are you receiving calls about this debt?

The answers to these questions will give you an indication of the degree of the problem you have and possible next steps. Are you truly ready to move toward resolution or continue to procrastinate?

- Do you want to do some or most of the work yourself or turn it over to someone else to help?
- Can you avoid letting the process get you down?
- Can you stay motivated to follow through?
- Are you willing to do the necessary homework to complete the job?
- Can you be disciplined about talking to collectors or loan servicers and working the details?

GETTING A PARTNER TO HELP

Depending on your situation, you may be okay with doing the work yourself. It depends on these factors:

- Are you current with your payments? If so, you may still choose to work with a qualified financial advisor to review your loans. They can do this in connection with your personal finances to evaluate how repayment fits your master financial plan. They may also share other available options for improvement that you may not be aware of.
- Are you struggling to make the payment but are current? If so, get professional help that includes your total financial picture.
- Are you behind or in default? Get your data together and contact your servicer about loan rehabilitation. They will work with you to help with the payment restructure (unlike a credit card debt collector), as they are incented to get your program in compliance. It's essential to get out of default.
- Simultaneously, consider getting professional advice.
- When seeking third-party advice, compare multiple options and be careful to document what you hear and who you speak with.

THE MENTAL AND EMOTIONAL DIMENSIONS OF STUDENT DEBT

Anxiety and Avoidance

It's not uncommon for many to avoid dealing with the uncomfortable or unknown. It's just too painful to address. The situation may seem impossible and hopeless. With student debt, the size of it can be so large that it appears there will never be a way out. Avoidance isn't in your best interest as it simply adds to the cost and increases anxiety and stress.

While in graduate school, many students told me they didn't know what they would owe after graduating or didn't want to think about it. It was as if they inherently knew it was a bad situation but chose to do nothing to plan for the inevitable repayment coming due.

Anxiety can be simply described as worry about the future. You're feeling a lack of control about the situation. It's filled with unknowns, and this creates fear and uncertainty.

The best solution can be to create your ideal vision of a positive future through planning and action. You'll do this by gathering information and then getting advice through some type of professional partnership.

First, establish a clear understanding of the details of your situation (remember about taking inventory of your loan details?). Start the process of getting good advice. These are two key steps that will reduce your financial anxiety because you'll have established some control over the situation and are taking constructive action.

Procrastination

Among the poor financial habits associated with debt problems are making late payments, forgetting due dates, ignoring the interest costs, and generally delaying addressing the issue. This procrastination contributes to increased interest and fees and often increases the overall balance.

With student loans, delaying filing the annual income and employer certifications (where applicable) can trigger costly problems. These processes are relatively simple and actually take very little time or sophistication to complete. Numerous resources are available to help as needed and mentioned throughout this chapter. You can put many of these tasks on reminders and autopilots to save money and reduce last-minute stress. Here are some tips:

- Add recurring calendar reminders for monthly student loan payments.
- Set up automatic deductions. Federal loans will generally reduce your interest rate if you do. Note this on your calendar a few days in advance so you're aware of the coming bank deduction.
- Add an annual student loan review in conjunction with your overall financial picture, goals, etc. Calendar and schedule this with a professional advisor.
- Schedule a few hours every quarter to review your financial goals. This will include actions around your student debt.

FIND PROFESSIONAL HELP!

You may want to turn your problem over to others to solve if you are willing to exchange money to do that. Here, we will discuss how you can make the most and wisest use of your money while working with a service provider to assist with your student loan problem.

In fact, one of my recommendations is that even if you don't believe you have a student debt problem, it would be wise to speak with a qualified professional to understand whether there are better options and strategies for effectively managing your student debt.

Many companies are vying to work for consumers with financial issues including student loans. Some claim to have access to "new government programs." Beware. While there are changes as noted in the section "Pandemic Pause," you should take a critical eye to companies that cold call you or have websites with no individuals listed with their financial credentials.

If you've searched the internet for a student loan solution, you'll see all sorts of promises marketing their form of help. Avoid completing website forms from these companies as these are lead generators, and they will sell your name to multiple companies who will hound you forever.

Hundreds, if not thousands, of companies spend millions on all forms of media advertising services to propose solutions to resolve back taxes, offer credit card debt solutions, and refinance student debt. So, where do you go? Who do you trust?

Since student loan problems are so pervasive, companies have been springing up over the last five years. Unfortunately, many take advantage of desperate consumers and provide little in the way of quality service or true relief while charging for items that could be done by you at no cost. If you receive an unsolicited call about your student debt, you've obviously been selected from a company that pulls lists of individuals who owe student loan debt from the credit bureau. Be very careful. In fact, hang up. Qualified professionals will not cold call you.

Watch out for companies that sell you on the idea that consolidation will help. Typically, it may be part of the solution, but without a personal financial review covering income, expenses, other debts, and some future projections, walk away. You want someone who will review all of your personal finances and look to have you as a long-term client, not a one-time sales event.

Also, avoid companies that charge monthly fees and promise to manage your student loans. The company entity you would pay any recurring fees to would be a financial planner (CFP) or one of the other licensed financial advisors. Their fees will be clearly disclosed, and you'll know what you are getting for the service.

So, what type of financial advisor should you choose to help with your student debt?

- A certified professional accountant (CPA)
- A certified financial planner (CFP)
- A qualified, fee-only investment advisor

Those are just a few to consider. You can verify their background and if there are any actions against them using the FINRA BrokerCheck at https://brokercheck.finra.org/.

You want a representative that has a fiduciary responsibility to act in your best interest. They are responsible for providing helpful advice and not for selling you things you don't need. Fiduciaries are legally obligated to work in your best interest.

When working with your personal finances, you need to get the best advice possible from someone specializing in personal finance. Think about it. You go to a physician when you have a physical issue. You go to a mechanic when you have a problem with your car. So, that's the first step; find someone who understands personal finance. And equally important, you should find someone who understands student loan debt.

Here's the challenge. With the multiple student loan programs available today and the measures available to solve problems, I would not recommend going to anyone who does not have broad-based experience helping clients with student loans and personal finance. Professionals who work in regulated industries such as financial planning and tax are good places to start.

VETTING YOUR FINANCIAL ADVISOR FOR HELP WITH STUDENT LOANS (AND FINANCIAL MANAGEMENT)

1. You can search the web and find financial advisors everywhere. Unfortunately, many of the websites look very similar and say much of the same thing. Run a search for financial advisors for student loans or certified student loan advisors to narrow down your results. For a company, look at the team section of their website and the individuals listed to see if there is any reference made to student loan help. You can also find a trained financial advisor who is certified

in student loan advising at CSLAInstitute.org. You can also do a general search for "CSLP student loan advisors."

2. At this point, you can fill out a contact form and tell them what you're interested in and that you want some comprehensive advice about student loan repayment and financial planning. Look for companies that can work in a digital environment, meaning if an advisor is in California, they can work with you in New York.

3. Your other option is to make the call and state what you're looking for. Describe your issues and questions. I've included a list of ten questions to ask before you choose a student loan advisor, including what you might say to kick things off correctly and save everyone time.

If you are having a conversation and get the sense that they believe student debt is just another debt like credit cards or a mortgage, stop there. As noted here, it's more complex. I'm sharing this because I want to help you eliminate someone who isn't well qualified.

In fact, you may get responses that say you're not a fit for their organization. The reason is simple, as they only work with very high income or net worth professionals focusing on investments. Some providers may work with only women who start businesses, while others may focus on early career professionals. You get the idea. Find someone whose ideal client is you and your situation.

I suggest you question the individual or company with the following series of questions. This is a big part of your life, and these simple questions should help you know right away if they are a good fit.

THE 10 CRITICAL QUESTIONS TO ASK BEFORE YOU CHOOSE A STUDENT LOAN ADVISOR

This checklist provides suggestions on choosing a financial advisor qualified to help with student loan repayment strategies as part of their overall financial plan.

Your student loans are part of your financial plan, impacting your ability to make other purchases, prepare for retirement, and plan for a business or family addition. You need to select an individual who knows finance and the complex, changing nature of student loans.

Question 1: *"Where did you gain your information about student loan advising?"*

- This is critical because they are helping you with what could be one of the most significant debts you may ever have. It pays to know something about the person you are using for critical financial decisions.
- Where did they get personal financial training?

Question 2: *"How do you stay informed about legal and program changes to student loan programs?"*

- Ideally, they will participate in a continuing education program that provides ongoing training and support.
- They need to stay updated on changes in government programs and financial training for their respective industries such as tax, financial planning, investments, or insurance.

Question 3: *"What professional designations do you have in finance?"*

- Good answers may include CPA, CFP, RIA, CLU, CFA, or EA. These indicate that they work with clients on personal financial planning and investments.
- Professional certifications usually indicate arduous training and assessment requirements.
- Look for experience advising clients on student loans and personal finance such as tax, investments, or insurance.

Question 4: *"How do you decide on the best program for my situation?"*

- Pay attention to what is said and your sense of what isn't said. Do you get the impression you are being sold something or that the person is looking out for your best interest?
- Ideally, they will talk to you about thoroughly assessing your financial situation, not just your student loans. They should ask about your present and future financial goals. Are you planning a family, starting a business? All of these factors can affect your repayment strategy.

Question 5: "Do you advise based on my short- and long-term financial goals? How?"

- Similar to the last question, find out how much they want to know about your goals. If they do not seem to care how your personal finances will change from year to year, such as with increases in your family income, they are probably not a good fit.

- Failure to account for present and future financial changes could end up significantly increasing the total cost of repaying your student loan debt.

Question 6: "What type of ongoing advice and support services do you provide?"

- Student loans take years to repay and require periodic evaluation based on life's changes. You'll want to have an advisor who will stick with you over time and help make decisions about potential program changes as well as discuss other financial decisions.

- Look for someone interested in a long-term relationship—not a one-time event. Many companies are out to sell you consolidations or file paperwork, and then they will disappear. You can do this on your own. Seek a long-term, professionally trained financial advisor who provides more.

Question 7: "How do my long-term goals align with my loan repayment strategy?"

- The repayment strategy you use works in conjunction with your personal financial goals. For many, the debt repayment is a sizeable monthly hit to the budget. Choosing the proper payment at the right time can make it easier to apply your income to the things that matter most (e.g., family planning, businesses, retirement, home purchase).

- Loan programs have forgiveness provisions. Your financial plan needs to account for that and any tax liabilities that can occur. Ask about how they can help if you are pursuing forgiveness.

Question 8: "What happens with my repayment plan if I get married?"

- Just ask the question and see if the answer is clear. They should explain the considerations on how your payments may be affected by marital status, where you live, and your family size.
- Another factor is if your new spouse has loans. You need someone who understands that this is a factor in calculating the best income-based repayment plan for you.
- A professional advisor should be able to provide specifics and will ask you about your present or future spouse and their student loan debt, their income, and your projected increases over the next few years.

Question 9: "How should I expect my balance to change over the repayment term?"

- Ideally, they can provide a schedule of your projected repayment plan. Not immediately but at another call, as this requires some analysis.
- They should explain how things will change over time, your total loan balance, and interest paid.
- Ask if they will provide a detailed loan analysis of several options with a repayment schedule. If not, perhaps this is not the advisor for you.

Question 10: "What effect will my plan have on other aspects of financial life?"

- As we have noted, student loan repayment affects your entire financial life and plans. If the person you are considering does not speak in detail about this, move on. They do not have your interest at heart and are probably not fully informed about how to help with all the implications of your loan repayment strategy. For example, if you have a well-tuned student loan repayment plan, more cash is free for other goals and that can be life-changing.
- Ensure your repayment plan includes consideration of other financial goals.
- Understand that your payments may or may not reduce the loan balance depending on the program. In fact, this may not matter if you are in a forgiveness program. Regardless, the impact of increasing debt must be considered alongside your financial goals.

IN SUMMARY

- Use only qualified advisors to assist with your student loan questions and repayment planning.
- Avoid call centers where you are dealing with unknown individuals having limited to no financial training.
- Use advisors who invest in themselves to learn more about personal finance and student loan repayment.
- Avoid fee-based solutions that only file documents. You can file documents at no cost. You are seeking an ongoing advisory relationship for best results.
- Seek out help who demonstrate that they have a strong understanding of student loans through professional designations and examples of experiences where they've helped others.
- Look for specific thoughtful answers. You will get a sense if they are interested in working with you.

THE COST OF REAL HELP

You may think a licensed financial advisor is too expensive. This is flawed thinking. A skilled financial professional can help with your student loan repayment planning in addition to providing other important financial advice. Think of this as an annual physical exam. You will find varied fees for service across the industry and just need to do some research using the information found in this chapter. After all, paying a little for quality guidance can ultimately save you money, time, stress, and anxiety.

A qualified financial advisor may charge for an analysis and a custom plan that includes your student loan solution.

Another reason to choose a qualified professional is that they have been certified based on rigorous standards and professional testing for knowledge. They won't have legal and BBB marks against them. You want a "financial surgeon" who's done their homework and is committed to helping clients. This requires serious, long-term preparation, sometimes years of study, and sitting in a monitored testing room for several hours, working through complex financial scenarios. Would you want to use that person or someone who cold calls you from a remote call center?

I advocate for having a comprehensive financial plan that includes your student debt, regardless of how much money you make today. Without a plan, you're floating and subject to the winds of change that blow you anywhere. A plan will provide direction and strategies to mitigate the challenges that inevitably come. The plan will take into consideration where you want to go, what you want to achieve with your financial resources, and a roadmap to get there.

If you're facing a tough financial challenge(s), you can overcome them. You can do this!! Just do it!

SUMMARY OF NEXT ACTIONS

- Inventory your student loans. First, pull your credit report. This will show you any private loans and their status. To get your federal loans, go to StudentAid.gov.
- Make a note of the type of loan, interest rate, payment, and term.
- Review your student loan finances now because of the changes (Fall 2021) in repayment programs.
- Place important dates on your calendar to remind you about completing an annual loan review.
- If you are in public service loan forgiveness, complete your annual employment certification.
- If you are in an income-driven repayment plan, complete your required income certifications. Note: You should do this whenever your income changes—up or down.
- Find a qualified financial advisor who can review your loans and personal finances to make sure you're on the best track to match your goals.
- Commit to a routine of making on time payments! If you are behind, get help by contacting your loan servicer.
- Find a qualified financial professional and commit to at least a 1 time per year review

- Keep a positive attitude that these actions are helping you make the most of managing your debt. You're no longer avoiding and procrastinating. You're having a financial success mindset.

ABOUT THE AUTHOR
Larry R. Taylor, Ph.D.

For over 20 years, **Larry** has provided a wide range of consulting services in healthcare, online learning, financial services, and SAS technology. His work frequently focuses on increasing the overall performance of digitally-focused businesses and intersects the disciplines of psychology, behavioral marketing, and technology. Larry has worked with numerous startups, Universities, and large organizations such as McKesson, Microsoft, and Becton Dickinson. He holds two master's degrees and a Ph.D. in psychology, emphasizing online media.

CONCLUSION

HEALING YOUR MINDSET WITH MONEY AND YOUR CREDIT

Mindset is a funny thing. Even when we fix the immediate problem—whether that's debt management, debt settlement, or bankruptcy—and even after we endure the painful process of eradicating our debt, the first thing most consumers want to know is how soon they can get credit again. They will always want the house, the car, and anything else that sets them apart from their peers. It's the rare exception when someone who's made it to the other side learns their lesson and vows to never put themselves in such a precarious financial standing again.

Chances are, no one has ever taught you how to have a relationship with your money. Yes, I said relationship.

When you're in a relationship and want it to last, you understand that it will take daily, focused attention to keep the spark alive. Every decision you make in terms of that relationship will have an effect. And if you ignore it or abuse it, that relationship will end, and it will end poorly.

It's the same thing with finances.

IT'S NEVER TOO LATE TO SALVAGE YOUR OWN RELATIONSHIP WITH MONEY

As you're in the process of working through your debt, consider making small changes to your financial mindset, starting with protocols you can start immediately, like setting up an automatic fund diversion—a direct deposit every one or two weeks into a savings account. If you don't see it, you can't spend it. Emergency funds are smart to build, too!

Remember that no matter what you were (or weren't) taught about money at a younger age, you can always learn new techniques and skillsets and adopt a more neutral or even a positive mindset around money.

Money doesn't make anyone evil.

Money doesn't make you better than or less than anyone else.

Money is simply a tool to support your lifestyle and family. That's it! And the more you learn about money and are able to remove any emotions from the equation, the easier it will become to manage it instead of it managing you.

Each one of us is a work in progress, especially when it comes to debt. Until then, we can continue to do the best we can with our current circumstances.

No matter your financial status now, you can always take one small step forward toward resolving debt, saving money, and shifting your mindset. Now that you better understand the debt industry and its many moving parts, you can begin to make smarter decisions based on your financial goals.

In fact, you can learn a great deal about money by reading books, taking online financial courses, and listening to podcasts. It's never too late to brush up on your financial literacy! Once you take the fear and uncertainty out of money and money management, your online bank accounts will no longer be a dark and scary place to visit.

Remember, you can't always predict big life events, and you can't always budget for unforeseen circumstances. But you can educate yourself, learn to control your spending, increase your savings, and think about your big purchases and financial goals in a new light.

TEACH YOUR KIDS ABOUT MONEY

A lot of parents give their kids an allowance, which is an excellent start. But what if you went further? What if you instituted a rule where they had to submit a spending report for the previous week in order to get their next allowance? It could show what they spent, what they saved, what they gifted, and what they tithed. What if you paid them in cash so that they'd have to physically deposit their funds? That way, they'd have a tactile connection to their money as well as a tactile separation from their money when it was spent.

That might sound a little overboard, but it really does work! Teaching kids about money at a young age—spending, saving, and the value of "things"—allows them to experiment, make mistakes, make their own decisions, and learn about money in a safe environment. That way, by the time they're old enough to get a credit card or a school loan, they will understand what they are signing up for and how to manage their money and their purchasing decisions wisely.

All too often, we send our teenagers to college and fill out their student loan forms for them, barely involving them in the process when it's ultimately *their debt* we're helping them to secure. So, what if, instead of simply asking them to sign here and there and once more right here, we discussed the terms with them? What if we talked to them about rates and payment schedules and how much that education would ultimately cost? What if we helped them feel invested—truly invested—in their futures?

I'll tell you what would happen. We'd raise the next generation to do better with their finances than we did with what little we were taught.

WHAT YOU CAN DO RIGHT NOW

- Now that you've made it to the end of the book, take another deep breath. Whew! You've taken a huge first step in taking your power back against the credit industry and in creating healthier financial habits.

- Take baby steps! You have to crawl before you walk, even when it comes to paying down debt. Consider making small changes to your financial practices, such as setting up a savings account, turning off automatic payments, and making your coffee instead of spending $8 a day at your local coffee house. It may seem small now, but it adds up quickly.

- Now that you better understand how credit—and money, in general—works, you can teach others and share tips that have worked for you. Even better, teach your children and grandchildren about money so they have a smart head start on finances.

ABOUT THE AUTHOR

Wade Torkelson is the cofounder of Reliant Payments. He is a visionary entrepreneur, and over the past twenty years, has founded numerous companies in the financial services industry. Prior to founding Reliant Account Management (RAM), Wade was a founding member of JH Portfolio Debt Equities from 2009–2013, which quickly grew to be one of the largest purchasers of charged-off credit card debt portfolios in the US. He also founded Persolvo Data Systems, a SaaS-based software platform that aggregated debt settlement account data, and went on to lead the company to rapid growth, ultimately accumulating over six billion dollars in aggregated account data by 2012.

Wade began his career in the financial services industry in 2000 by founding Homeland Financial Services and grew it to one of the largest debt settlement providers by 2005. Today, he is recognized as a leading subject matter expert on the debt settlement industry and the receivables management industry and regularly consults with clients across both industries.

But more importantly, Wade is a husband, father, grandfather, and proud dog dad of Roxy the Boxer. He and his wife, Christina, live outside of Nashville, Tennessee.

ACKNOWLEDGMENTS

To my wife, Christina, thank you for all your help and expertise in writing this book. I could not have done it without you.

To Mark A. Carey, Esq. and Larry R. Taylor, PhD, thank you for your time, your hard work, and for contributing detailed chapters that explain often-difficult topics.

To Hasnain Walji, thank you for adding in your expertise on wellness, nutrition, and mindset to this book--which will make a huge difference in many ways to the readers.

To my incredible book team: Thanks to brilliant Alice Sullivan for getting the words out of my head, to the awesome editorial duo of Terry Stafford and Sissi Haner for polishing them, to design genius Dino Marino for getting the cover and interior just right, and to my book strategist Honorée Corder for pulling it all together.

APPENDIX:

Inventory of Student Loans Checklist and Other Resources

ADDITIONAL RESOURCE LINKS

StudentAid.gov

For videos, infographics, and other federal student aid publications, visit StudentAid.gov/resources.

REPAY YOUR LOANS

Get information about managing repayment of your federal student loans at StudentAid.gov/repay.

FINANCIAL AID FOR GRADUATE AND PROFESSIONAL DEGREE STUDENTS

Are you planning to go to graduate or professional school but need help paying for your education? See StudentAid.gov/grad.

BROKER CHECK: CHECKS FOR VALID LICENSES AND VIOLATIONS

BrokerCheck.Finra.org

INVENTORY OF LOANS CHECKLIST

Begin by gathering the following information:

1. Get your **federal student loan** record.
   - Visit StudentAid.gov.
   - Click the Financial Aid Review button.
   - Log in using your Federal Student Aid ID (FSA ID). If you do not already have an FSA ID, select the "Create Account" button.

   Step 1: Enter a username and password.

   Step 2: Enter your Social Security number, name, and date of birth and five challenge questions and answers.

   Step 3: Submit your FSA ID application.
   - Click to download the .txt file.

2. **Private student loan** inventory
   - Visit AnnualCreditReport.com and fill out the request form.
   - Download credit report.
   - Note balance and status of all student loans listed on credit report that are also not included in the NSLDS record of federal loans—these are your private student loans.

3. Optional additional information (available from loan servicers – private and federal)
   - Current monthly payment dollar amount (not applicable if you are still in school)
   - Current repayment plan and length of repayment term (not applicable if you are still in school)
   - For private loans:

     o Current interest rates

     o Whether the interest rates are fixed or variable

     o If variable, whether the interest rates have any caps, and if so, what they are

     o Copies of the Promissory Notes

GLOSSARY OF TERMS

Active debt. Debt one has to physically take action to obtain, such as credit card debt, student loans, auto loans, and mortgages.

Avalanche method. A method of prioritizing one's debt with the highest interest rates; the most effective method number-wise.

Bankruptcy. A way to eliminate or reorganize debt once one has become delinquent on their credit card bills; created for people who cannot pay their creditors under the original terms that were set to quickly end the cycle.

Bankruptcy Abuse Prevention and Consumer Protection Act (BAPCPA). An act passed in 2005 that introduced new requirements for bankruptcy and made it more difficult to declare personal bankruptcy.

Chapter 7 bankruptcy ("liquidation bankruptcy"). A form of bankruptcy where the court takes legal possession of one's property and appoints a bankruptcy trustee who sells nonexempt properties to repay creditors.

Chapter 13 bankruptcy ("reorganization bankruptcy" or "the wage earner's plan"). A form of bankruptcy for those who do not qualify for a Chapter 7 bankruptcy and who make enough money to make payments to their creditors; administered by the court trustee.

Charge-off. When a creditor closes an account to future charges to sell it to a debt buyer or transfer it to a collection agency; the borrower is still legally obligated to repay the debt.

Collateral. A piece of property pledged as security for repayment of a loan; to be forfeited in the event of a default.

Collections. A term used by a business when referring to money owed to that business. When a customer does not pay the business within the terms specified, the bill amount becomes past due and is sometimes submitted to a collection agency.

Compound interest. The interest on a loan or deposit calculated based on both the initial principal and the accumulated interest from previous periods.

Consumer Financial Protection Bureau (CFPB). A bureau that assesses how debt settlement affects consumers and possesses rule-making authority, meaning they propose and enact rules that the credit industry must abide by.

Credit limit. The maximum amount of money a lender will allow a consumer to spend using a credit card or revolving line of credit.

Credit line. An amount of credit extended to a borrower.

Credit report. A detailed summary of an individual's credit history prepared by a credit bureau.

Credit Reporting Agency (CRA) ("credit bureau"). An organization that collects and researches individual credit information and sells it to creditors for a fee so they can make decisions about granting loans.

Credit score. A number assigned to a person that indicates their capacity to repay a loan.

Credit utilization ratio. The amount of revolving credit one is currently using divided by the total amount of revolving credit they have available.

Creditor. A person or company to whom money is owed.

Debt buyer. A company that purchases delinquent or charged-off debt from creditors at a discount.

Debt disruptor. An industry insider who believes consumers are being taken advantage of and analyzes how they procured debt.

Debt validation. A process completed by credit repair companies to prove the borrower owes money by directly asking the creditor; validation could include personal information or the original signed contract.

Delinquent. When one is behind on payments. Once one is delinquent for a certain period of time, the lender will declare the loan to be in default, and the entire loan balance will become due at that time.

Depreciate. A reduction in the value of an asset with the passage of time.

Dunning letter. A collection letter received by mail that must be written with specific language and certain disclosures. If one receives a letter that is not written with the right disclosures, their rights are violated.

Early charge-off. An ability of banks to begin negotiations before ninety days have passed.

Equity. A company's total assets minus its total liabilities.

Fair Credit Reporting Act (FCRA). The law that governs how a CRA and one's creditors handle their credit information.

Fair Debt Collection Practices Act (FDCPA). An act that provides a list of things a debt collector cannot do when attempting to collect a debt. The list includes things that are considered abusive, deceptive, or unfair.

FDIC Credit Card Activity Manual. A manual consisting of twenty sections, a supremely helpful glossary, and two appendices of legalese that regulates every rule by which every bank must abide; it governs what credit card companies can do and when they can do it.

Federal Deposit Insurance Corporation (FDIC). An organization in charge of how the banks handle consumers and credit cards, in addition to the Office of the Comptroller of the Currency (OCC).

Federal student loan. A loan underwritten by the federal government to assist students with educational expenses. It includes features that can help borrowers with medical problems, job loss or other income reduction. Each loan comes with a set of standard terms and an interest rate that's applicable at the time of issue. As the student progresses through school, additional loans are added based on the current federal student loan interest rate.

Federal Trade Commission (FTC). An independent agency of the United States government whose job it is to oversee the banking and credit industry to make sure the consumer is not taken advantage of.

FICO score. The result of all the information in one's credit history. It determines the deal a lender will make including the amount one can borrow, the length of time to repay it, and the interest rates.

First-party/Original creditor. The bank or other lending institution that loaned the money or extended the credit.

Furnishers. Entities that supply credit reporting agencies (CRAs) with information.

Garnishment. When the government takes money from one's tax returns, wages, bank accounts, etc.

Hard inquiry/hard credit report pull. Occurs when purchasing a car or mortgaging a house; actions that set off an alarm on one's credit report and immediately deducts points. From that point, most bureaus won't continue to ding one's credit score for a set period of time, so creditors can check their scores as many times as necessary while they shop for a home or car.

Hardship. A legitimate disruption or displacement within one's income; an occurrence in one's life that prohibits them from working.

Income-Driven Repayment. A group of student loan repayment programs where your payments are based on your income, state of residence, and family size.

Interchange fee. The fee charged by banks to the merchant who processes a credit card or debit card payment. The purpose of the fee is to cover the costs associated with accepting, processing, and authorizing card transactions.

Interest rate. The amount of interest due per period as a proportion of the amount loaned, deposited, or borrowed.

Letter of dispute/validation. A document you can send to the credit bureaus to point out inaccuracies on your credit reports and to request the removal of the errors.

Liquidate. Converting property or assets into cash or cash equivalents by selling them on the open market.

Loan consolidation. Taking multiple debts, applying for a loan, getting approved for that loan, then paying off all the others to consolidate the debt into one loan with simple interest.

National Foundation for Credit Counseling (NFCC). An organization overseen by the OCC that regulates what can and cannot be offered to the consumer.

Office of the Comptroller of the Currency (OCC). An organization in charge of how the banks handle consumers and credit cards, in addition to the Federal Deposit Insurance Corporation (FDIC), and oversees the NFCC.

Passive debt. A debt owed after an unforeseen event that's out of one's control, such as a medical expense.

Penalty rate. An extremely high interest rate charged by credit card issuers when a borrower violates the card's terms and conditions. The penalty rate is triggered most often when cardholders are late making monthly payments.

Periodic interest rate. The annual percentage rate divided by 365.

Placement. The first time the original creditor sends your account to a collection agency it is called first placement. When they recall it and send it out a second time, it is called second placement. When they recall it and send it out a third time, it's called tertiary. Normally, after the third placement, they will pull it back, let it sit, and decide what they want to do. They may sell it as tertiary paper to someone and the price dictates the worth of the debt.

Portfolio. When a bank issues a certain type of credit. A portfolio contains different individuals' money obtained from mutual funds, pension funds, and hedge funds so that the bank's money is not necessarily at risk.

Principal. The money one originally agrees to pay back before interest is added.

Private student loan. A loan underwritten by a privately-owned lender to assist students with educational expenses. It generally requires more interaction with creditors, can be costly in terms of fees and interest, and requires good credit.

R9. When a lender charges off one's debt as a loss and inflicts the worst damage to their credit score at the six-month point of nonpayment.

Re-age. When one reports old debts as newer than they are.

Rule-making authority. A power the CFPB possesses, meaning they don't rely on Congress to pass new laws.

Secured loan. A loan in which the borrower pledges some asset as collateral for the loan, which then becomes a secured debt owed to the creditor.

Snowball method. Dave Ramsey's method of paying off smaller debts first; the snowball method offers more opportunities for positive reinforcement and sets up an environment of wins that often do create a slow but steady result.

Soft credit report pull. When a creditor wants to offer someone a store card or needs to make sure they qualify, or if one's employer or landlord runs a credit check. These soft credit report pulls are solely for marketing purposes and have no impact on one's credit.

Statute of limitations. A law that sets the maximum amount of time that parties involved in a dispute have to initiate legal proceedings from the date of an alleged offense.

Telephone Consumer Protection Act (TCPA). A federal statute that prohibits all autodialed or prerecorded calls or text messages to one's cell phone. The statute also applies to landlines and fax machines for the purpose of telemarketing calls.

Thin-file clients. Those with no history of servicing or paying back debt because they have never operated in a debt environment. The credit reporting agencies do not have information on these consumers, so they cannot rate them as a credit risk.

Third-party creditor (A collection agency). A person or entity—usually a collection agency—who was not a party to one's agreement with the bank.

Tradeline. A record of activity for any type of credit extended to a borrower and reported to a credit reporting agency. A trade line is established on a borrower's credit report when a borrower is approved for credit, and it records all activity associated with an account.

Unbanked/Underbanked. Individuals who may have a bank account but do not write checks. Instead, they cash their checks at the bank and operate strictly off of cash, using money transfer services like PayPal to send money when necessary.

Unsecured loan. A loan that does not involve collateral, including credit cards, personal loans, and student loans.

Wallet share. A marketing metric used to calculate the percentage of a customer's spending for a type of product or service that goes to a particular company. Wallet share fluctuates over time and changes with the economy.

Warehouse. When a bank does not take immediate action on a debt once the account is in post charge-off.

INDEX

A

Advisor 153, 156, 160, 161, 163, 164, 166, 167, 168, 169
Alcohol 138, 140
Annual 24, 27, 33, 58, 96, 161, 168, 169
Annual fee 27, 33
Anxiety 131, 133, 135, 137, 139, 140, 141, 142, 144
Application 88, 107, 109, 114, 115, 124, 155
Avalanche method 13, 178

B

Balance vi, 12, 20, 21, 24, 25, 27, 30, 32, 33, 34, 37, 39, 43, 58, 59, 63, 65, 74, 75, 77, 86, 93, 94, 95, 96, 100, 101, 129, 148, 161, 167, 177
Bankruptcy iii, v, vi, vii, 3, 6, 7, 13, 22, 35, 47, 53, 54, 62, 67, 72, 79, 82, 83, 84, 85, 86, 87, 88, 89, 90, 91, 94, 120, 122, 152, 156, 171
Bankruptcy Abuse Prevention and Consumer Protection Act of 2005 (BAPCPA) 83
Bankruptcy Act of 1867 83
Bankruptcy Act of 1898 83
Bankruptcy Acts 83

C

CARES Act 154

Certified financial planner (CFP) 158, 163

Certified public accountant (CPA) 158

CFP. *See also* Certified Financial Planner

Chapter 7 53, 67, 82, 84, 85, 88, 89, 90, 91, 178

Chapter 13 82, 84, 87, 88, 89, 90, 91, 178

Charge-off 12, 34, 35, 36, 64, 77, 94, 95, 96, 178

  Early 178

Collateral 16, 17

Collateral 178

Collections v, 17, 34, 36, 37, 39, 41, 42, 48, 62, 73, 74, 76, 82, 84, 104, 108, 115, 116, 125, 153, 179

Collections agency. *See also* Third-party creditor

Collector iv, 64, 92, 96, 97, 99, 100, 105, 111, 112, 113, 114, 115, 116, 117, 123, 125, 126, 160

Compound 4, 56, 60, 71

compound interest 4, 56, 60

Compound interest 179

Consolidation vii, 54, 55, 56, 57, 59, 60, 61, 66, 69, 151, 152, 162

Consumer Financial Protection Bureau (CFPB) 109, 179

Consumer rights 117, 118, 130

Contingency fee 112

COVID-19 72, 154

CPA 158, 163, 165. *See* Certified public accountant

Credit card i, ii, iii, v, vi, vii, viii, 1, 3, 4, 5, 6, 7, 8, 13, 16, 17, 18, 19, 20, 22, 23, 24, 25, 26, 28, 30, 31, 32, 33, 34, 36, 39, 40, 41, 43, 48, 49, 55, 56, 58, 59, 60, 61, 65, 70, 72, 73, 74, 75, 78, 79, 82, 86, 94, 98, 100, 108, 110, 111, 119, 127, 128, 129, 150, 151, 152, 156, 160, 162, 173, 174

Credit counseling vii, 13, 17, 18, 45, 46, 53, 56, 59, 62, 63, 64, 65, 66, 68, 84, 88, 90

Credit limit i, 17, 22, 179

Credit line 19, 20, 27, 28, 60, 86, 179

Creditor ii, iv, 6, 12, 17, 20, 26, 37, 38, 41, 44, 45, 46, 52, 53, 54, 63, 71, 75, 76, 80, 82, 83, 84, 92, 94, 98, 101, 103, 110, 111, 114, 119, 120, 121, 122, 123, 125, 151, 179

Credit report 10, 12, 20, 21, 26, 27, 30, 37, 38, 41, 52, 57, 66, 67, 79, 84, 85, 86, 88, 94, 98, 119, 120, 121, 122, 123, 169

Credit Reporting Agency (CRA) 118, 179

Credit score 1, 5, 7, 18, 19, 20, 21, 22, 26, 27, 30, 36, 40, 41, 45, 55, 57, 61, 64, 66, 70, 72, 73, 78, 86, 100, 103, 119, 122, 149

Credit utilization ratio 27, 179

CSLAInstitute.org 149, 164

D

Dave Ramsey 13, 101, 182

Debt i, ii, iii, iv, v, vi, vii, 1, 2, 3, 4, 5, 6, 7, 8, 9, 10, 11, 12, 13, 14, 15, 16, 17, 18, 19, 20, 21, 22, 23, 24, 25, 27, 28, 30, 34, 35, 36, 37, 38, 39, 40, 41, 42, 43, 44, 45, 46, 48, 49, 53, 55, 56, 57, 58, 59, 60, 62, 63, 64, 65, 66, 67, 69, 70, 71, 72, 73, 74, 75, 76, 77, 78, 79, 80, 81, 82, 83, 84, 85, 86, 87, 89, 90, 91, 92, 93, 94, 95, 96, 97, 98, 99, 100, 101, 102, 103, 104, 105, 106, 108, 111, 112, 113, 114, 115, 116, 117, 120, 121, 122, 123, 124, 125, 126, 127, 129, 130, 146, 147, 148, 149, 150, 151, 153, 154, 156, 157, 158, 159, 160, 161, 162, 163, 164, 166, 167, 169, 170, 171, 172, 173, 174, 175

  Active 3, 22 178, 179, 180

  Buyer 3, 22, 92, 111, 178, 179, 180

Debt collector 96, 97, 99, 100, 105, 111, 113, 114, 115, 116, 117, 123, 125, 126, 160, 180

Default 22, 41, 42, 43, 49, 57, 63, 73, 80, 126, 128, 155, 160

Delinquency 65, 96, 147, 149

Delinquent 8, 12, 25, 42, 48, 62, 73, 74, 82, 84, 94, 96, 119, 126, 149, 151

Demographic 39

Department of Education 154, 155

Depreciate 179

Depressed 133, 136

Depression 137, 139, 140, 141

Diet 139, 140, 141

Direct 114, 171

DOE 154, 155. *See* Department of Education

Drugs 138

Dunning letter 180

E

Early ii, 12, 64, 72, 83, 164

Early charge-off ii, 12, 64, 72, 83, 164, 180

Emotional health 132, 137, 138, 141, 143, 144

Equity 22, 56, 57, 58, 85

Exercise(s) 143

Experian 15, 23, 26, 82, 118, 123, 149

Extended Repayment 150

F

Fair Credit Reporting Act 89, 118, 180

Fair Debt Collection Practices Act 112, 130, 180

FCC 124

FCRA 118, 119, 120, 180

FCRA Violations 120, 121, 122, 127

FDCPA 112, 113, 114, 118, 127, 130, 180

FDIC iii, 8, 39, 73, 180, 181

FDIC Credit Card Activity Manual 180

Federal iii, 19, 23, 37, 42, 72, 83, 109, 110, 118, 119, 123, 124, 149, 150, 151, 152, 153, 154, 155, 156, 157, 161, 169, 177

Federal Communications Commission (FCC) 124

Federal Deposit Insurance Corporation (FDIC) iii, 180, 181

Federal Family Education Loan 154

Federal Family Education Loan (FFEL) Program Forgiveness 154, 155

Federal loan 151, 153

Federally backed loan. *See* Federal loan

Federal student loan(s) 149, 154, 157, 180

Federal Trade Commission 19, 109, 124, 180

FedLoan Servicing 154

Fee i, 27, 33, 100, 104, 112, 116, 163, 168

FFEL 154, 155. See Federal Family Education Loan Program

FICO score 19, 29, 180

Fiduciary 163

Fight or Flight 134, 135, 139

Financial advisor(s) 80, 153, 156, 160, 162, 163, 164, 166, 168, 169

Financial hardship 152

Financial health 136, 138

Financial planning 67, 163, 164, 165

Financial stress 131, 134, 136, 137, 138, 140, 141, 142, 143

Financing 152, 153

FINRA BrokerCheck 163

First-party creditor 92. *See also* Federal Family Education Loan Program; *See also* Original creditor

First placement 76

Forgiveness 153, 154, 155, 157, 166, 167, 169, 170

Form 1099 129, 157

FTC 109, 180

Furnishers 120, 121

G

Garnishment 80

Graduated repayment 150

Graduate students 148

H

Hard credit report pull. *See also* Hard inquiry

Hard inquiry 27. *See also* Hard credit report pull

Hardship 8, 12, 13, 14, 38, 39, 40, 43, 70, 71, 76, 77, 105, 152

Headaches 131

I

IBR 150. *See* Income-Based Repayment

ICR 150

Income-based repayment 150, 156, 167

Income-Contingent Repayment 150

Income-driven repayment 148, 169

Insolvency 156

Interchange fee(s) 23, 33

Interest iv, 4, 10, 11, 12, 13, 16, 17, 19, 22, 23, 24, 25, 26, 32, 33, 34, 46, 53, 55, 56, 57, 58, 59, 60, 61, 63, 64, 65, 67, 71, 77, 79, 81, 85, 86, 88, 92, 94, 95, 108, 109, 110, 113, 119, 128, 148, 150, 151, 152, 153, 154, 159, 160, 161, 163, 165, 167, 169

Investment 146, 163

IRS 129, 156, 157

L

Letter of dispute 38
Letter of validation 98
Liquidate 10, 53, 86, 89, 90, 101
Liquidation 84, 85, 88, 90, 94
Loan vii, 3, 5, 10, 11, 16, 17, 21, 40, 41, 48, 54, 55, 56, 57, 58, 59, 60, 61, 66, 67, 69, 73, 85, 86, 99, 108, 110, 115, 119, 124, 128, 129, 146, 147, 148, 149, 150, 151, 152, 153, 154, 156, 157, 158, 159, 160, 161, 162, 163, 164, 165, 166, 167, 168, 169, 170, 173, 177, 178, 179, 180, 181, 182, 183
Loan forgiveness 153, 157, 169

M

Mental health 132, 133, 136, 137, 142
Merchant fee 33
Mindset iv, 1, 2, 3, 6, 7, 8, 9, 12, 13, 14, 44, 47, 53, 67, 70, 71, 81, 100, 158, 170, 171, 172
Monetary settlement 129
MyFedLoan.org 154. *See* FedLoan Servicing

N

National Do Not Call Registry 124, 130. See Robocalls
National Foundation for Credit Counseling (NFCC) 63

O

OCC iii, 8, 39, 63, 64
Office of the Comptroller of the Currency (OCC) iii
Original creditor 38, 76, 98, 110, 111. *See* First-party creditor

P

Pandemic 47, 72, 154, 162

Passive 20, 21, 46

Passive debt 20, 21

Pay As You Earn 150

PAYE 150. *See* Pay As You Earn

Payment restructure 160

Penalty rate 40, 78

Periodic 24, 86, 166

Periodic interest rate 24

Perkins Loan Program 154

Personal 6, 9, 10, 14, 22, 23, 24, 27, 35, 38, 39, 45, 46, 48, 59, 65, 73, 80, 84, 85, 86, 96, 99, 100, 109, 111, 112, 115, 116, 117, 127, 147, 151, 152, 153, 160, 162, 163, 165, 166, 168, 169, 170

Personal information 38, 127

Placement 76, 77

Portfolio 8, 37, 48, 49, 62, 76, 93, 94, 111, 174, 182

Primary loan 55, 150

Principal 24, 42, 59, 64, 74, 86

Private 125, 151, 152, 153, 169, 177

Private loan financing 152, 153

Private student loan 177

PSLF 154, 155. *See* Public Service Loan Forgiveness

Psychology of student loan debt 147

Public Service Loan Forgiveness (PSLF) 154, 155, 157, 169

R

R9 36, 64

Rate(s) ii, 4, 8, 10, 11, 12, 13, 16, 17, 19, 22, 23, 24, 26, 39, 40, 46, 49, 56, 57, 58, 60, 61, 63, 64, 66, 67, 71, 78, 79, 85, 86, 88, 89, 93, 108, 109, 119, 128, 149, 151, 152, 153, 159, 161, 169, 173

Re-age 8, 65

Re-aging 8, 120

Reassign 53, 89

Refinancing 66, 152, 153

Rehabilitation 160

REPAYE 150. *See* Revised Pay As You Earn

Repayment 17, 34, 35, 42, 48, 63, 64, 65, 71, 84, 85, 89, 90, 106, 147, 148, 149, 150, 151, 154, 156, 160, 164, 165, 166, 167, 168, 169

Repayment strategy 147, 148, 165, 166, 167

Resources 1, 7, 86, 104, 150, 156, 158, 161, 169, 176

Retirement iv, 39, 53, 88, 148, 164, 166

Revised Pay As You Earn (REPAYE) 150

Robocalls 123, 124, 130

    National Do Not Call Registry 124

S

Second placement 76

Secured 17, 20, 22, 58, 84, 87

Secured loan 17

Self-worth 131, 132, 136, 143

Servicer 49, 154, 156, 160, 169, 170. *See* Student Loan Servicer

Settlement program 42, 78, 84, 95

Sleep 132, 135, 138, 140, 141

Snowball 13, 40, 56, 101, 102, 109

Snowball method 13

Soft pull 26

Statute 37, 65, 79, 114, 116, 119, 123, 127

Statute of limitations 37, 65

Stress 131, 132, 133, 134, 135, 136, 137, 138, 139, 140, 141, 142, 143, 144

Studentaid.gov 153, 154, 155, 169, 176, 177

Student loan 5, 129, 146, 147, 148, 152, 153, 154, 156, 157, 158, 161, 162, 163, 164, 165, 166, 167, 168, 169, 173

Suicidal thoughts 131

Suicide 137, 144

Supplements 141

T

TCPA 123, 125, 130. *See* Telephone Consumer Protection Act

Telephone Consumer Protection Act (TCPA) 123, 130

Tension 131

Tertiary 76, 77

Thin-file clients 23

Third-party creditor 110, 111. *See also* Collection agency

Third-party creditor student loan 5, 129, 146, 147, 148, 152, 153, 154, 156, 157, 158, 161, 162, 163, 164, 165, 166, 167, 168, 169, 173, 177

Tradeline 26

U

Unbanked 23
Underbanked 23
Unsecured 3, 16, 58, 73, 84, 87, 100, 147
Unsecured loan 16
US Student Loan Debt Statistics 146

V

Validation 38, 97, 98, 113, 127
Violations 127, 130
Vitamins 140, 141

W

Waiver 154, 155
Wallet share 6, 7
Warehouse 35

Y

Yoga 143